# COUNTERING WMD

## THE LIBYAN EXPERIENCE

ROBERT G. JOSEPH

National Institute Press, 2009 ©

Published by
National Institute Press
9302 Lee Highway, Suite 750
Fairfax, Virginia 20121

Library of Congress Cataloging-in-Publication Data (TK)

Joseph, Robert G.
 Countering WMD : the Libyan experience / Robert G. Joseph.
    p. cm.
 Includes bibliographical references and index.
 1. Nuclear disarmament--Libya. 2. Weapons of mass destruction--Gov-
ernment policy--United States--Case studies. I. Title. II. Title: Countering
weapons of mass destruction.
 JZ5665.J67 2009
 327.1'74709612--dc22

                              2008050549

ISBN 978-0-9776221-9-1

10 9 8 7 6 5 4 3 2 1

# *Dedication*

To the members of the Intelligence Community who made success with Libya possible.

# Table of Contents

## *Appendix*

# *Foreword*

In *The Libyan Experience*, Ambassador Robert Joseph provides the first publicly available inside account of the interactions that led to perhaps the greatest counterproliferation success of our time: the decision by Colonel Qadaffi to abandon his WMD and longer-range missile programs. Here is the actual history presented by a key figure involved throughout the process of the secret discussions that led to this dramatic outcome. The narrative is both scholarly and highly-readable; at times it is as much a real-life thriller as it is an historical text. As only a direct participant can, he describes the interactions with the Libyans and assesses their implications. This is the definitive story that now is told thanks to the author's intrepid work and to his meticulous accounting and assessment of events. This is a case study that is profoundly important to our understanding of proliferation, and of the tools and processes most helpful to its prevention and rollback. As such, it makes a major contribution to our future.

*Dr. Keith Payne*
*President, National Institute for Public Policy*

# *Preface*

> Today in Tripoli, the leader of Libya, Colonel Moammar al-Ghadafi, publicly confirmed his commitment to disclose and dismantle all weapons of mass destruction programs in his country. ...The United States and our allies are applying a broad and active strategy to address the challenges of proliferation, through diplomacy and through the decisive actions that are sometimes needed. We've enhanced our intelligence capabilities in order to trace dangerous weapons activities. We've organized a Proliferation Security Initiative to interdict dangerous materials and technologies in transit. We've insisted on multilateral approaches like that in North Korea to confront threats...
>
> Our understanding with Libya came about through quiet diplomacy. It is a result, however, of policies and principles declared to all. Over the last two years, a great coalition of nations has come together to oppose terror and to oppose the spread of weapons of mass destruction. We've been clear in our purposes. We have shown resolve. In word and in action, we have clarified the choices left to potential adversaries.
>
> President George W. Bush
> December 19, 2003

This book presents a case study of Libya's decision to eliminate its nuclear and chemical weapons programs, as well as its longer-range ballistic missile delivery capability. Three central questions are addressed:

- Why did Libya decide to abandon its weapons of mass destruction (WMD) and longer-range missile programs?

- What are the most significant "lessons learned" from the Libyan experience?
- How have other states pursuing WMD capabilities responded to Libya's decision?

The case study is intended to serve several purposes. First, the lessons learned from the Libyan experience may demonstrate how we can improve our overall counterproliferation strategy in key areas such as interdiction and declaratory policy. Second, the lessons learned may provide a foundation of knowledge and insight that can be applied to encourage or compel the leaderships of other proliferant states to pursue cooperative disarmament and abandon their WMD and longer-range missile programs. Third, the study will present for the record the facts of the Libyan experience which, to date, have often been misunderstood or misrepresented.

# I. Executive Summary: From Tripoli to Tennessee

## *The Setting*

Libya's decision to abandon its nuclear and chemical weapons programs, as well as its longer-range missile capabilities, is best understood in the context of the Bush Administration's determination to counter the growing threat from proliferation. This determination, evident at the outset of the President's first term in office, was reflected in: (1) the articulation of the first National Strategy to Combat Weapons of Mass Destruction (WMD); (2) the Administration's successful non- and counterproliferation initiatives; and (3) the innovative use of intelligence and other national and multilateral tools to disrupt and defeat proliferation threats from hostile states and non-state networks.

## *Articulating the Strategy*

President Bush understood from the start that success in protecting against contemporary WMD threats would require a fundamental change in how the United States and other countries perceive the proliferation challenge and respond to it. Traditional nonproliferation measures, while essential, were not sufficient to prevent, and did little to protect against, this complex set of threats. Within the U.S. Government, this meant that it would no longer be sufficient to react to proliferation after the fact with political condemnations and economic sanctions. Instead, proactive measures must be taken to prevent and roll back proliferation. That included a requirement for new concepts of, and capabilities for, deterrence, dissuasion, and defense to deal with the full range of WMD threats.

 Consistent with this view, the President immediately began to establish a new framework to combat modern WMD and missile threats, putting in place a comprehensive strategy involving proactive diplomacy, actions to counter proliferation directly, and better means for organizing and equipping the United States and its friends and allies to respond to the use of such weapons. The message was clear to all: the United States was serious in its determination to prevent and protect against these threats, and would use all of its tools – diplomatic, economic, scientific/technological, and military – to achieve this goal.

In December 2002, the Administration published the National Strategy to Combat Weapons of Mass Destruction. The document identified three major pillars of the strategy:

- Protection or counterproliferation, including interdiction, deterrence, and defense.
- Prevention or nonproliferation, including support for regimes such as the Nuclear Nonproliferation Treaty (NPT) and the Chemical and Biological Weapons Conventions (CWC and BWC), increased Cooperative Threat Reduction (CTR) efforts, greater controls on nuclear materials, export controls, and sanctions.
- Improved capabilities for response or WMD consequence management.

To integrate the pillars, the strategy called for improvements in several key enabling functions, including: intelligence collection and analysis; research and development; international cooperation; and tailored strategies against state and non-state proliferators.

Promulgated publicly at the time the United States was leading the international effort within and outside of the United Nations Security Council (UNSC) to compel Iraq to account for its WMD programs and activities, the National Strategy received substantial attention in the U.S. and foreign press. While the coverage differed from country to country, one theme was constant: the United States would no longer tolerate the continued proliferation of WMD and missiles by hostile states.

## *Promoting Effective International Initiatives*

To implement the national strategy, the President initiated a highly visible, diplomatic campaign to encourage other states to join the effort to prevent and protect against WMD proliferation. In 2002, he successfully proposed within the G-8 the establishment of the Global Partnership Against the Proliferation of Weapons and Materials of Mass Destruction, with the goal of providing $20 billion over 10 years for threat reduction and nonproliferation projects. In May 2003, the President announced a second initiative that drew worldwide attention. Made public at a press conference in Poland, the Proliferation Security Initiative (PSI) would create an impressive coalition of states to stop the trade in proliferation materials and equipment through proactive enforcement of national and international authorities.

In the counterproliferation field, a number of initiatives to develop improved capabilities for deterrence and defense against WMD threats also received wide attention in the international press. Following the September 11 attacks and the subsequent anthrax crimes, several steps were taken in the biodefense field, including funding of new medical countermeasures in the Bioshield program and the expansion of vaccinations of U.S. forces against smallpox and anthrax. Missile defense was another key priority to bolster deterrence and protection against states like North Korea and Iran. The U.S. withdrawal from the Anti-Ballistic Missile (ABM) Treaty and the President's public announcement that the United States would deploy a defense of all 50 states against a North Korean-type ballistic missile attack made headlines around the globe.

Another much-publicized priority was adapting U.S. nuclear forces to the new security environment, reflected in the Administration's Nuclear Posture Review (NPR). The NPR specifically updated U.S. strategic planning to help address the new threats posed by proliferation. Administration briefings and unauthorized leaks of the findings and recommendations of the Review were covered extensively in the foreign media. A May 2003 report in the Libyan press noted: "In its nuclear posture review of 2001, the Administration urged development of a wide range of new nuclear capabilities, and said the U.S. might, in some circumstances, use nuclear weapons against countries that do not have them: Syria, Libya, Iran and Iraq." Despite its inaccuracies, this and other reports in the Libyan press undoubtedly resonated with the Libyan leadership.

As with the public articulation of a comprehensive strategy to combat proliferation, putting in place effective multilateral initiatives such as PSI and acquiring new capabilities to deter and defend against WMD showed the seriousness with which the Bush Administration pursued the goal of combating WMD and missile proliferation. The President was direct in stating publicly his commitment to develop the counterproliferation capabilities needed to deter and defend against WMD threats. In this way, while increasing U.S. national efforts to prevent proliferation in the first instance, the President added a new dimension to combat WMD and their means of delivery. Interdiction would block proliferation directly and produce incontrovertible evidence of its attempt. The threat of the use of force to defend U.S. security meant that those who illicitly pursued these weapons must consider carefully the risks inherent in their actions. Both of these factors would play directly on the Libyan decision to abandon WMD and longer-range missiles.

## *Disrupting and Defeating WMD Threats*

Libya asked to meet with U.S. and United Kingdom (UK) officials to "clear the air" about WMD programs in Libya only days before the invasion of Iraq in March 2003. That invasion followed more than six months of intense diplomatic maneuvering at the UN in New York and in the Middle East and Gulf region. President Bush and Prime Minister Blair were the leading advocates behind the effort to compel Saddam to account for the chemical, biological, and nuclear materials that U.S. and UK intelligence agencies assessed remained hidden by more than a decade of Iraqi denial and deception. There was general agreement that Iraq's actions constituted material breach of numerous UNSC resolutions going back more than a decade. The President and Prime Minister emphasized their determination to enforce these resolutions and hold Iraq accountable on WMD, even if force was required. The U.S. and UK position was clear: Saddam needed to make a strategic choice. Either he could choose to cooperate fully with international inspectors and provide a complete and accurate accounting of Iraq's programs, or he would be removed from power.

The buildup of hundreds of thousands of U.S., UK and other coalition troops sent a tough message not only to Baghdad, but to others who sought WMD, especially in the region. The President's words — that those who seek such weapons will put their security at risk — were being backed by action. In Libya, which had long possessed chemical weapons and had embarked on a large-scale clandestine effort to be able to enrich uranium for nuclear weapons, the message was clearly received. The immediate concern of the Libyan leadership was that, after Iraq, it would be the next target for U.S. military action. This concern may well have been aggravated in the late fall of 2002 by stories in the international press, sourced to Israeli Prime Minister Sharon, that Iraq had sent a number of its nuclear physicists to Libya to work on a joint weapons program.

Additional factors appeared to converge in early 2003 that may have aggravated Tripoli's concern that, after Iraq, Libya would be next. One was Washington's stepped-up campaign in January to deny Libya the chairmanship of the UN Commission on Human Rights. Another may have been press stories based on unclassified Central Intelligence Agency (CIA) reports and testimony that U.S. intelligence believed Libya, described as a state sponsor of terror, was expanding its nuclear infrastructure and pursuing chemical and biological weapons capabilities. Together, these and other actions taken by the United States in the region suggested to the Libyan leadership that the United States would seek "regime change" in Libya. While the Bush Administration had not formally adopted regime change in Libya as an active policy goal, the concern was perceived as real and served as a motivation for Colonel Qadaffi to reach out to the United States.

In reaching out in early 2003, Qadaffi sought accommodation on two key issues of central importance to the United States. First, in a January interview with *Newsweek*, he stressed that support in the Arab world for Osama bin Laden was a threat not just to the United States but also to his own rule. Noting that he was a target of an al-Qaeda assassination attempt, he indicated that Libyan intelligence would cooperate to "wipe out" this threat through the exchange of information with the United States and Great Britain. Second, in March, Qadaffi embarked on a secret WMD initiative; his son, Saif al-Islam, approached the United States through British contacts for a dialogue on WMD. While intimating that "everything would be on the table" and that Libya would be willing to renounce WMD, absent from the Libyan request was any commitment to abandon programs that Tripoli publicly continued to deny existed. In fact, Libya formally continued to reject claims by U.S. intelligence that it was seeking WMD. In January 2003, Libyan Foreign Ministry spokesperson, Hassouna al-Shawesh, emphasizing that Libya was a signatory of the NPT, dismissed a U.S. charge that it was building a nuclear infrastructure: "These are allegations the CIA habitually puts out to serve interests hostile to the peoples" of other states. Given this posture, the March 2003 request to "clear the air" was more likely an attempt to hedge against what was seen as a potential liability to the regime, than a signal of intent to abandon WMD programs.

## *The Timeline*

On December 19, 2003, Colonel Qadaffi announced that Libya had voluntarily decided to give up its nuclear and chemical weapons programs and missiles with ranges over 300 km, making clear that he now believed that these weapons programs no longer added to Libya's security or well-being. In March 2004, the ship, *Industrial Challenger*, arrived in the United States with over 500 metric tons of cargo – including everything from centrifuges to Libya's 800 km-range Scud C force. This marked an end to Tripoli's nuclear weapons program and its possession of longer-range missiles, arguably the most significant nonproliferation achievement to date.

It is useful to recognize a number of key milestones between Libya's initial overture in March 2003 and Qadaffi's strategic decision to abandon WMD and longer-range missiles.

**April 2003**: The first meeting of U.S., UK, and Libyan intelligence personnel is held with discussion of the need for a technical visit to Libya by U.S. and UK experts; no agreement is reached. Musa Kusa, chief of Libyan external intelligence, is the principal point of contact for Libya, and remains so throughout the process.

**August 2003**: Agreement is reached within intelligence channels to meet with Colonel Qadaffi to discuss the prospect for technical visits.

**September 2003**: A U.S./UK meeting is held in Tripoli with Colonel Qadaffi during which he agrees in principle to allow a technical visit, but defers to his senior subordinates to work out the details. No date for a technical visit is agreed upon during the follow-on discussions.

**October 3, 2003**: Interdiction of the ship, *BBC China,* en route to Libya: five large 40-foot shipping containers marked "used machine parts" are offloaded in an Italian port and are determined to contain thousands of centrifuge parts manufactured in Malaysia by the A.Q. Khan nuclear proliferation network.

**October 7, 2003**: Evidence of a centrifuge program is laid out to the Libyans; Tripoli immediately agrees to dates for the visit of a U.S./UK technical team.

**October 19-29, 2003**: First U.S./UK technical team conducts on-site visit.

**November 2003**: U.S./UK meeting is held following the completion of the first technical visit. The Libyans are presented with additional intelligence concerning their nuclear program. Arrangements are finalized for the second technical visit.

**December 1-12, 2003**: U.S./UK technical team conducts second on-site visit. During the first visit of the technical team, much was learned about Libya's WMD and missile programs. By the end of the second visit, the Libyans:

- Admit having a nuclear weapons program and having bought uranium hexafluoride feed material for gas centrifuge enrichment.
- Acknowledge having made about 25 tons of mustard chemical weapon agent, as well as aerial bombs for the mustard, and small amounts of nerve agent.
- Agree to inspections by the International Atomic Energy Agency (IAEA) and the Organization for the Prohibition of Chemical Weapons (OPCW), and to abide by the

range limitations of the Missile Technology Control Regime (MTCR).

Perhaps most encouraging, as well as most disturbing, at the end of the second visit the Libyans delivered nuclear weapons design materials acquired from A.Q. Khan. These materials were described as possessing an alarming level of detail, identifying everything necessary to make a nuclear bomb.

While a number of questions remained even after the return of the experts in December, U.S. and UK intelligence assessments concluded that Libya was in fact coming clean about its WMD and missile activities. Moreover, both intelligence services believed that the best means of addressing outstanding issues was to deepen the engagement with Libya (through U.S. and UK experts, as well as through the OPCW and IAEA), thus allowing further access to Libyan personnel and facilities. On this basis, the decision was made to proceed to policy discussions.

**December 16, 2003**: First U.S./UK policy discussion with Libyan officials. The opening statement by the Libyan side, emphasizing the need to remove sanctions, moved backwards from previous commitments. U.S. and UK representatives emphasized that the purpose of the meeting was not to negotiate specific steps or responses to Libyan actions on the part of the United States and United Kingdom. At the same time, U.S. and UK participants made clear that, if Libya did move forward with its commitment to end its WMD and longer-range missile programs, one major barrier to improved relations would be removed.

After the opening comments, the representatives held almost six hours of tense discussions focused primarily on the draft text for a public Libyan statement. Libyan participants initially resisted any explicit mention of the existence of Libya's WMD programs or a commitment to eliminate them. U.S./UK representatives insisted that such references be included.

The discussion of the Libyan statement was followed by an even more frank discussion of specific actions Libya would need to take to eliminate its WMD and longer-range missile programs. The U.S. side, supported by the United Kingdom, raised the requirement for an explicit commitment from the Libyan delegation to eliminate WMD and missile programs, and emphasized the need for agreement at the table by the Libyan representatives to the following commitments:

> *Nuclear:* (1) removal of all materials and equipment related to the nuclear weapons programs: all centrifuges and all parts and associated equipment; all uranium hexafluoride (UF6) and other nuclear materials; all uranium conversion equipment; all documentation; (2) signature and implementation of the Additional Protocol to the safeguards agreement with the IAEA.

> *Chemical:* (1) elimination and destruction of all chemical agents, munitions, and equipment; (2) complete accession to the CWC.

> *Biological:* (1) complete access to, and monitoring of, all related facilities; (2) formal commitment not to pursue biological weapons capabilities.

> *Missiles:* (1) removal of all ballistic missiles with a range greater than 300 km, as well as all associated equipment; 2) no development or deployment of ballistic missiles with a range greater than 300 km; (3) adherence to the parameters of the MTCR.

The U.S. and UK representatives made clear that Libyan agreement to these precise commitments was essential if there was to be a successful outcome. Although initially reluctant, the Libyan participants agreed to each point, and to the explicit requirement for international monitoring and verification in all WMD and missile areas.

While each of these commitments was important, two were unique and precedent-setting. The first was the removal of all components of the nuclear program. This was essential to avoid a future problem if Tripoli were to argue later that equipment acquired for activities such as uranium conversion or even enrichment could be retained for a "peaceful" nuclear program. The Iran case, of cynically manipulating the provisions of the NPT to acquire sensitive technologies for weapons purposes under the guise of a peaceful program, was very much present in the minds of the U.S. and UK participants. Confirming that this was a real possibility, Saif al-Islam stated publicly on December 20, one day after the announcement of the Libyan decision, that "Of course, this program could be used for peaceful purposes." However, by this time, the commitment to the removal of all such equipment had been agreed to and announced. The second unique and precedent-setting commitment was the elimination of missile capabilities beyond the MTCR parameter of 300 km range, for which Libya had no legal or political obligations.

For their part, the Libyan participants emphasized the importance of characterizing their decision to abandon WMD and longer-range missiles as "voluntary" and in Libya's self-interest. U.S. and UK representatives were quick to agree that this was accurate and should be done.

**December 18, 2003:** When the meeting on December 16 ended, it was unclear how Colonel Qadaffi would react to the draft statement hammered out over the table. To encourage Libyan acceptance of the statement, and to get final buy-in from Qadaffi, Prime Minister Blair reached out to the Libyan leader. In an unprecedented conversation between these two men, Colonel Qadaffi reportedly was concerned that the Libyan decision would be portrayed as caving into pressure, as well as about the even greater vulnerability of Libya to attack now that it had revealed its WMD programs to the United States and United Kingdom. According to press reports, the Prime Minister gave assurances that a Libyan statement — if clear on possession and elimination — would be met with positive statements by the Prime Minister and President.

In a conversation following the call with Colonel Qadaffi, President Bush and Prime Minister Blair reportedly exchanged views on next steps. Both agreed that any Libyan announcement must be explicit as to the existence of WMD programs and the commitment to abandon them, and that Colonel Qadaffi must make it clear that he personally authorized the Libyan statement. Both also appear to have agreed that U.S. and UK responses to an acceptable Libyan announcement would make it evident that there would be positive steps if Libya did end its WMD programs.

Following these two conversations, the Libyans provided two alternative drafts of a statement to be made by the Libyan Foreign Minister. They informed the United States and United Kingdom that, if either one of the two versions was acceptable, Tripoli would broadcast it the next day. They also noted that, if Washington and London could not agree to either text, the Libyans would be content to have the United States and United Kingdom announce Libya's decision and Tripoli would not deny it.

**December 19, 2003:** Neither of the two Libyan versions from December 18 was considered by the United States and the United Kingdom sufficiently precise in acknowledging WMD programs and making a clear commitment to eliminate them. Through the UK channel in Tripoli, Washington and London provided inputs to the language that would correct these deficiencies. Yet another draft was received from Libya in mid-afternoon Washington time. This version came close to what was required. A final brief exchange produced agreement on what all three sides could accept, including references to centrifuge and chemical weapons programs and an explicit obligation for immediate international inspections — including monitoring of Libya's missile force — to meet its elimination commitments.

For the next several hours, U.S. and UK officials were in constant contact awaiting confirmation of the Libyan statements. During this time, the Libyans sent word to Washington and London that Qadaffi's statement would be released in written form. Although a last-minute change from what had been expected to be an in-person announcement, this was considered acceptable — a necessary face-saving step by Colonel Qadaffi.

The wait extended well into the afternoon Washington time, late evening in London. Finally, confirmation was received that the Libyan statements had been made. The statement by the Libyan Foreign Minister conformed to the agreed upon text; the statement released in the name of Colonel Qadaffi was also sufficient to meet the requirements. Once confirmed, Prime Minister Blair and President Bush made their separate but coordinated announcements.

## *Libya's Motivations*

Libya's investment in its WMD and missile programs was substantial — in terms of financial resources, the involvement of many civilian and military personnel, and the perception that such capabilities contributed to national security and prestige. Giving up these programs would not be easy or without risk.

Multiple motivations were in play as the Libyan leadership worked through the decision to abandon WMD and longer-range missile programs. One was the desire to end U.S. economic and political sanctions, which had a substantial effect on Libya's economy and sense of isolation. Over the course of five years, Tripoli had taken a number of steps to achieve the lifting of UN sanctions, and sought to accomplish the same with the United States. Most significantly, Libya reached a settlement with the families of the victims of Pan Am 103 in March 2003. There is no evidence to suggest, however, that the goal of ending sanctions would have been sufficient to induce Libya to acknowledge, remove, and destroy its WMD programs. All evidence suggests that other motives were essential to this outcome.

As discussed above, the timing of the Libyan approach to the United States and United Kingdom, coming as hundreds of thousands of coalition forces were being deployed to the region to enforce UN Security Council resolutions on Iraqi WMD, was more than coincidental. In fact, Colonel Qadaffi reportedly explained to congressional delegations in January and March 2004 that, "one of the reasons... he was giving up the weapons [of mass destruction] was he did not want to be a Saddam Hussein, and he did not want his people to be subjected to the military efforts that were being put forth in Iraq." Earlier, in September 2003, Italian Prime Minister Berlusconi noted in a press interview that Qadaffi told him even more directly: "I will do whatever the United States wants, because I saw what happened in Iraq, and I was afraid."

Likewise, it is not by accident that the Libyan leadership agreed to a specific date for U.S. and United Kingdom experts to enter the country immediately upon the presentation of evidence from the interdiction of the *BBC China*. This dramatic action demonstrated both the existence of a nuclear weapons program, as well as the ability of the United States and United Kingdom to disrupt the critical supply line on which Libya depended. This would have a double effect on Tripoli's calculations: first, it drove down the prospect for success of the nuclear program; and, second, it increased the risk of U.S. and UK military action because doubts no longer remained about Libyan intent and actions.

Without the use of force in Iraq and the successful interdiction of the *BBC China*, the outcome almost surely would have been different. While Libya may have decided to give up some capabilities, such as its chemical weapons program, it is unlikely that it would have agreed to the removal of all elements of its nuclear program or its longer-range missiles. As suggested by Qadaffi's son, Tripoli could have argued that its investment in uranium enrichment was for peaceful purposes and retained the equipment in country, and could have resisted any restrictions on its missile force, as it had no legal or political constraints against developing and deploying such missile capabilities.

Discussions with senior Libyans revealed additional underlying motivations. For several years, the Libyans waged their own battle with Islamic extremists, mostly the Libyan Islamic Fighting Group, who had sworn to destroy the Qadaffi regime. Having observed the U.S. reaction to September 11, the war in Afghanistan, and the preparation for war in Iraq, the Libyans believed that only the United States was strong enough and determined enough to strike back against Islamic terrorism. The Libyans believed they needed to align themselves with the United States against Islamic extremism because they were no longer sure they could defeat their extremist enemy alone.

Finally, based on comments by senior Libyans, it appeared that senior Libyan leadership, including Colonel Qadaffi and members of his inner circle, had begun to assess their legacy and were disturbed by what they saw. Their isolation from the West had imposed substantial costs, as Libyan society was stunted in its economic and educational growth. The journey through pan-Arabism and pan-Africanism had not been successful, and the impending removal of Saddam Hussein only highlighted the fragility of dictatorial governments and the risks of pursuing WMD while a designated adversary of the United States. The WMD programs had not provided Libya with the additional strength and stature that could help overcome all of the other shortcomings. For this reason, it became apparent to some that these programs needed to be ended in order to move the society forward.

A net assessment of Libyan perceptions and motivations suggests heightened costs in the ongoing pursuit of WMD, lowered value in the acquisition of these weapons, and sharp risks in continued hostility toward the United States. U.S. and UK commitments to improved relations following Libyan abandonment of WMD and longer-range missiles represented considerable value for Colonel Qadaffi under this set of circumstances.

# Lessons Learned

## Demonstrate Seriousness

From the outset of the Administration, the President emphasized the priority he placed on countering the proliferation of WMD and missiles, and his determination to combat this growing threat through all necessary means.  His first major national security address in May 2001, four months before the September 11 terrorist attacks, not only identified WMD and missile proliferation as the major threat to the United States, but made evident the need to adopt new strategies and develop new counterproliferation capabilities to meet this threat. This message was reinforced and magnified after September 11, as reflected in the President's speeches at The Citadel and West Point.

The National Security Strategy, published in September 2002, and the National Strategy to Combat Weapons of Mass Destruction provided both the purpose and blueprint for action that the Administration would follow to prevent and protect against proliferation.  The message was clear to all proliferators: the United States considered the spread of weapons of mass destruction and their possession by hostile states and terrorists to be a call for action. The nexus of proliferation and state sponsorship of terror, such as that found in Libya, was highlighted by the President as a particular concern.

In this context, the message to rogue states pursuing WMD and missile capabilities was explicit:  these weapons will not contribute to security but will have the opposite effect.  This message was clearly transmitted and, in the case of Libya, clearly received. The Libyan announcement on December 19 noted: "Libya's belief is that an arms race does not serve its security nor the security of the region, but conflicts with Libya's great concern for the world blessed with security and peace."  Later, Colonel Qadaffi would make this point even more directly:  "We made this step owing to a conviction of ours, that is because this programme is not useful to Libya, but it actually represents a danger and a threat to Libya's very integrity."

## Insist on a Strategic Decision

At the time of the initial Libyan approach in March 2003 to "clear the air" on WMD, U.S. and UK officials were skeptical of Libyan motivations and intentions. Given the timing of the approach, it appeared that Libya's leadership was likely making a tactical move to hedge its position without committing to the elimination of these programs.

Between March and October 2003, while this skepticism would remain, there was a sustained attempt to encourage Libya to be more forthcoming. But the Libyan reluctance to allow U.S. and UK experts into the country was viewed as an indication that the leadership had yet to make a strategic decision to abandon WMD capabilities. U.S. and UK participants believed that only a strategic decision expressed by Colonel Qadaffi would produce the desired result by ensuring complete transparency into the history of the programs and full confidence in the elimination process. Moreover, it was agreed that the mode of operation must be insistence on a near-term strategic decision vice the long-term negotiating process characteristic of classic disarmament negotiations.

While the interdiction of the Libyan centrifuge parts in October 2003 led to agreement on dates to permit U.S. and UK experts into the country, the Libyan leadership at that time had not sought to implement the necessary strategic decision. On the ground, there was only an incremental opening up of the Libyan programs to the U.S. and UK experts. By the end of the second visit in December, the Libyans had acknowledged the existence of chemical weapons and a nuclear weapons program, as well as a longer-range Scud C force, and had indicated a willingness to eliminate these weapons and programs. But even then, more needed to be done.

It was not until the initial policy meeting on December 16, 2003 that Libya formally and explicitly agreed to the requirement that it both publicly acknowledge its WMD programs and commit to their elimination. Even at that meeting, the Libyan opening statement suggested Tripoli would resist any reference in its public statement to actual programs or to their elimination.

Yet, the U.S. and UK participants believed that, without such a public acknowledgement and commitment, the strategic decision was absent or would be easily reversible. Confidence that Libya had made the necessary strategic decision came only with the Libyan statement on December 19. Even then, the President's remarks made clear the intent to "trust but verify." The President stated that, while the Libyan decision was in itself a "development of great importance," it was still necessary for Tripoli to demonstrate "its seriousness" and "good faith" by meeting its commitment to complete and verifiable elimination of its WMD and longer-range missile programs.

## Employ All Tools

The Libyan experience demonstrates the requirement to employ all available tools to combat WMD proliferation – from diplomacy, to sanctions, to interdiction, to the use of intelligence and military power. In particular, the willingness to employ force against Iraq to enforce UN Security Council resolutions on WMD had a clear impact on the Libyan leadership.

Another tool that clearly contributed to the Libyan decision was the interdiction of centrifuge parts bound for Libya on the *BBC China*. Without the evidence provided by this interdiction, Libyan delay in permitting the visit of U.S. and UK experts likely would have continued. In turn, it was the knowledge of Libyan programs acquired by these teams that led to the full disclosure of the Libyan WMD and longer-range missile programs. And once disclosed, the prospective difficulties, costs, and risks of nuclear acquisition increased dramatically because the programs could no longer be pursued unnoticed. As a result, the pressure on Libya to agree to abandonment increased substantially.

The decision to use selected portions of collected intelligence to demonstrate to the Libyans the U.S./UK depth of knowledge of their WMD programs was also crucial in convincing Tripoli to abandon the programs. At times the Libyans were visibly disturbed by what they were told, but they appeared to develop significant respect for the U.S. and UK collection efforts, enhancing the credibility of the U.S. and UK participants, and leading to the conclusion that the programs could not be conducted in secret.

During the course of the engagement with the Libyans, U.S participants would become more aware of the significant impact of two other tools on the Libyan representatives. The first was declaratory policy — the powerful message of resolve conveyed by the words and actions of the Administration. The second was the importance the Libyans accorded to the prospect of educational opportunities in the United States for their scientists and students. The majority of the program directors in Libya had studied in the United States, and highly valued this experience. The most powerful Libyan participant, Musa Kusa, also spoke enthusiastically about his years as a university student in the United States.

## Create the Perception and Reality of a Win-Win Outcome

U.S. and UK participants were conscious from the beginning of the need to structure the outcome on a win-win basis: a nonproliferation victory for the United States and United Kingdom, as well as a political and national security victory for Libya. There was a common view that, were Libya to acknowledge and abandon these programs, it was necessary that its leaders could portray the outcome — in perception and fact — as contributing to Libya's own welfare and national security.

Moreover, U.S. and UK participants understood that a win-win outcome would produce a second path, different from that of Iraq, for other proliferators to follow. This would send the powerful message that, if these countries also were to abandon WMD programs, explicitly and verifiably, there would be benefits. In the case of Libya, the United States and United Kingdom made clear that abandonment of these programs would remove a major obstacle to the improvement of relations. At the same time, U.S. and UK participants emphasized that there were other impediments that needed to be addressed before the removal of sanctions, especially Libyan support for terrorism.

In his December 19 announcement, the President emphasized the more general point that Libya provided a new model for others to follow: "And another message should be equally clear: leaders who abandon the pursuit of chemical, biological and nuclear weapons, and the means to deliver them, will find an open path to better relations with the United States and other free nations." This same point was also included in the Libyan statement: "Libya's desire of this initiative is that all states will follow Libya's model, beginning with the Middle East region without double standards."

The message of a second model was readily accepted and promoted by the Libyan government. In early January, the editor of the Libyan news agency emphasized that, "with this bold decision, the great Jamahiriyah [Libya] has proved that it is the initiator and the motivator of the countries of the world to get rid of the programs and weapons of mass destruction, on the basis of its important and leading role in building a new world free of these internationally banned weapons and any kind of terrorism." That the Libyan decision had created a second model was also accepted by others in the region. An early January 2004 article in Cairo's *Al-Ahram* notes:

> Washington seems to have offered the leaders of the region two models to choose from: The Iraqi model with its deposed president Saddam Husayn — he fought the U.S. power and refused to cooperate with it and ultimately ended up the way he did — and the Libyan model of eliminating banned weapons voluntarily, integrating Libya in the international community, and ultimately receiving rewards, both direct and indirect.

Ensuring that Libya would benefit from taking the right course, and thereby making clear to others that there was an alternative model that they too could pursue to their benefit, became a priority for the United States and United Kingdom. Within a year, Libya would begin to gain substantially from its WMD decision as U.S. sanctions were lifted and political relations with the United States were restored. By January 2005, a number of economic and political steps had been taken which, together marked a profound positive change for Libya. In response to Libyan steps to eliminate its chemical, nuclear, and longer-range missile programs, the President lifted the national emergency imposed under the International Emergency Economic Powers Act, ended Executive Order sanctions, and terminated the applicability of the Iran-Libya Sanctions Act. These actions removed restrictions on travel, trade and investment, and ended many disincentives for American companies interested in undertaking business ventures in Libya. Moreover, Libyan assets in the United States were "unfrozen" with over

$1 billion being transferred back to Libyan ownership.

On the political front, a number of steps were taken by the United States: direct diplomatic relations were re-established with Tripoli; the first meeting in 25 years took place in 2004 between the U.S. Secretary of State and his Libyan counterpart; travel restrictions on Libyan diplomats in the United States were removed; and, bilateral exchanges were initiated in the areas of health and education. The visits of Prime Minister Blair and others to Libya, including President Berlusconi and Spanish Prime Minister Aznar, also demonstrated the value of Tripoli's actions to eliminate WMD and longer-range missile programs. Similarly, the invitation extended to Colonel Qadaffi for meetings with the European Union (EU) in Brussels, and the EU decision to lift its arms embargo, reflected the importance of Libya's abandonment of WMD capabilities.

## Be Conscious of Face

While firm in their dealings with the Libyans in both intelligence and policy channels, U.S. and UK participants always were conscious that a Libyan decision to abandon WMD and longer-range missile programs would have to be voluntary and would be very difficult. By some estimates these programs had cost Libya between $100 and $200 million and involved the careers of many in Libya's military and scientific community. Giving them up would entail a degree of political risk, even given the nature of the regime. This perception of cost and risk can be seen in a public comment by Colonel Qadaffi: "If you declare you have a programme for building nuclear or chemical weapons, if you declare this before the entire world, well, this requires courage. Those who possess these weapons do not declare it, exactly because they do not have the courage."

In the first policy discussion, the Libyans emphasized, and U.S. and UK participants supported, the need to characterize Libya's decision as "voluntary." The capture of Saddam only three days before this meeting — and the images of the former dictator flashed around the world — undoubtedly reinforced the conclusion of Libya's leaders that it was in their interest to abandon WMD programs. However, these images also made it more important from Tripoli's perspective that the decision not be construed as giving in to U.S. pressure. All three sides shared the view that, if an agreement were seen as a wholesale defeat for Colonel Qadaffi, its prospects would be much reduced as Qadaffi's prestige would be undermined at home and in the broader Arab community.

Predictably, a number of opposition figures and a few governments — notably Iran and North Korea — criticized the Libyan decision as an act of capitulation to avoid the fate of Saddam. However, this criticism received relatively little attention and had little noticeable impact. By speaking with a single voice in emphasizing the voluntary nature of the decision, the United States, United Kingdom, and Libya preempted those who would seek to use the decision for internal political purposes or to deny the applicability of the model to their own WMD programs.

## Ensure Direct Access to Leadership

Another essential ingredient for success was direct access to, and the personal involvement of, the three government leaders. All three considered the outcome a national security priority, and were willing to invest their personal effort and accept the risk of failure. As a result, the participants from each of the three countries were confident that their counterparts had direct access to, and were operating under instructions from, the highest level.

For the United States and the United Kingdom, President Bush and Prime Minister Blair remained intensely interested and closely involved throughout the course of the discussions. They were briefed at each step by those intelligence officers participating with the Libyans. They provided policy direction and, in so doing, made clear to all the importance they assigned to the outcome, and the requirement for secrecy. The President and Prime Minister were also willing to engage with Colonel Qadaffi, including by sending messages through the intelligence envoys.

As stated by the Libyan participants, only Qadaffi could make the strategic decision to acknowledge and abandon the Libyan WMD and longer-range missile programs. At each critical juncture, his advisors went to him for decisions which he made with caution and a degree of risk. It was clear from the Libyan participants that they would have preferred not to have taken to their leader the tough decisions that the U.S. and UK sides made necessary. They did so only because it was made evident that such decisions were integral to accomplishing their assigned task.

## Ensure Complete and Continuing Access for Verification

The Libyan experience makes evident once again that illicit activities by a state willing to violate its treaty commitments and IAEA safeguards obligations are not likely to be detected by international monitoring of declared activities. Inspections conducted by the IAEA, based on visits to declared sites, had led the Agency to judge that there was no evidence of Libya pursuing a nuclear weapons program. Following Tripoli's strategic decision to abandon its weapons program, the Libyans provided U.S. and UK experts access to additional sites associated with its nuclear weapons program. The undeclared activities at these secret locations demonstrated that IAEA safeguards cannot uncover clandestine programs. While the Additional Protocol provides the Agency with more authority to pursue undeclared activities, the Agency still must rely on the cooperation of the inspected state. It is not an intelligence organization. It has neither the authority nor resources to undertake the mission of detecting covert programs. The Agency's defensive reaction to Libya's announcement that it would abandon its nuclear weapons program spoke volumes about the limits of what should be expected of the Agency's capabilities, as well as the Agency's unwillingness to acknowledge those limits.

These limitations were evident to the United States and United Kingdom. Throughout the discussions with the Libyans, U.S. and UK intelligence and policy participants emphasized the need for full disclosure and transparency. By the end of the second expert visit, there were still unanswered questions and remaining concerns, but also a sense of astonishment about how much the Libyans had revealed. The assessment was that sufficient confidence existed to move forward on the policy side, and that even greater confidence would result from the continuing work with the Libyans both on a trilateral basis, as well as from Libya's cooperation with the OPCW and IAEA.

## Ensure Secrecy

Conducting the U.S./UK/Libyan dialogue and site visits in secrecy was an absolute prerequisite for success. Any hint of these activities leaked to the media almost certainly would have produced a different outcome. Had the fact of trilateral contacts been revealed publicly, the "angle" played up by the opposition — and likely reflected in the Arab and western press — would have been that Colonel Qadaffi was "running scared" to avoid the fate of Saddam. If confronted with this type of news story about abandoning WMD programs, Qadaffi would have been placed in a defensive position. Opposition to abandonment would have mobilized both internally within Libya and externally, especially within the Arab media.

For this reason, operational knowledge of the contacts with Libya was tightly restricted from the beginning. Within the Intelligence Community, there was a strict "need-to-know" rule applied. At the National Security Council (NSC), only a few individuals were involved. At State and Defense, knowledge was restricted to the very top level, and what was revealed was general in nature. Operational details, including the fact of the policy negotiations, were not shared with either department; other departments were unaware. Guidance came directly from the President. Policy (from the NSC) and Intelligence worked closely at each step to implement the President's direction.

## Act Fast

Perhaps a corollary to the need for ensuring secrecy, U.S. and UK participants understood that speed was essential. A drawn-out process clearly would have increased the prospects for press leaks. Moreover, once the first team was granted access to visit Libya, any delay in moving forward might decrease the pressure on the Libyan leadership, and allow time for opposition to mobilize internally and within the region. For this reason, following the second site visit in December, U.S. and UK participants pushed for the policy meeting within a few days and, once that meeting achieved the objective of a Libyan agreement to acknowledge publicly and abandon its WMD programs, pushed for an early public announcement by the three leaders. The pace in December — moving from the second site visit to the statements by the three leaders — was remarkable by any standard of diplomacy.

## Avoid Bargaining

A number of Libyan officials have asserted that the decision by Tripoli to abandon its WMD and longer-range missile programs was the outcome of intense bargaining in which the United States and United Kingdom agreed to compensate Libya in a direct and substantial manner. Such assertions, although often cited by others without direct knowledge of the secret dialogue, simply were incorrect.

As noted, the Libyan delegation opened the first policy discussion with a statement that emphasized the need to lift U.S. sanctions on Libya. U.S. and UK representatives responded directly that the discussion of sanctions was not the purpose of the meeting and that it would be premature to engage on this subject. U.S. and UK representatives emphasized the need to resolve the WMD issue by recording what must be a strategic decision to eliminate these programs.

From the outset U.S. and UK participants took the position that the very process of bargaining would undercut prospects for a clear and clean outcome; bargaining would slow down the process and likely cause confusion. Efforts to portray the process otherwise, including by Saif al-Islam, are inaccurate. (Saif noted in an interview on December 20, 2003 that, "The truth is that this initiative is a political deal. This is not a secret. It is a political deal; give and take. We give you this much and you give me this much.") More accurate is Colonel Qadaffi's observation that there was no "concrete reward" for giving up the nuclear program. Instead of negotiating X for Y, U.S. and UK representatives insisted that Libya acknowledge and abandon its WMD and longer-range missile programs. In doing so, they also made clear that Libya would remove a major obstacle to improved relations and greater economic and political benefits.

## Observations on the Policy/Intelligence Nexus

The intelligence channel proved to be the best operational vehicle for engagement with Libya as it is inherently compartmented, and can be fast-moving and flexible. It provided U.S. and UK policy-makers with an avenue that allowed direct access to Libyan leadership and timely feedback from the Libyans as each step unfolded.

Collaboration between U.S. and UK intelligence was critical to policy success. Working together as a team significantly increased the resources available to the task. Clandestine collection was increased as each service brought its sources to bear, and combining experience and skill proved invaluable in moving discussions with the Libyans forward. At the same time, close engagement with the Libyans was crucial. The flexibility of the intelligence channel allowed for continuous contact so that key decision points were pressed forward and the seriousness and urgency of the effort was emphasized over and over.

Throughout the Libyan operation, the operational and analytical synergy generated by operators and analysts working side by side was also critical to its successful policy outcome. This integration contributed to the vetting of clandestine sources and helped analysts question and reconsider their assessments as necessary. This was particularly important when the teams entered Libya for the first time in October 2003.

In the Libya case, disruption of supply-chain procurement proved essential to success as these operations provided important information and, in turn, leverage for the confident advancement of the policy agenda. This was essential to offset the limitations of technical and national collection efforts. Collection efforts revealed what the Libyans had in their nuclear program, but there was insufficient information to determine how the Libyans intended to exploit their nuclear materials. In the chemical program, the information that was collected was good, but the projected quantity of chemical weapons was inaccurate. Prior to the U.S./UK team visits to the various WMD sites, more clandestine sources with access to various facilities would have been more valuable than additional technical collection.

Lastly, the intangible concept of operational flow proved once again to be important. The combination of instincts and solid judgment born of operational experience, the acceptance of risk, and the commitment of leadership to success allowed for timely decisions during each of the key engagements with the Libyans. In the intelligence channel, these intangibles should not be underestimated.

# II. The Setting: Getting Tough on Proliferation

In the intervening five years, Libya's decision to abandon its WMD and longer-range missile programs often has been portrayed as either the consequence of gradual internal political change or as the delayed culmination of an earlier Libyan initiative, dating back a decade or more. The first portrayal is so general as to be of little analytical merit. The second appears less than serious given that the Libyan nuclear weapons program expanded significantly from the 1990s until 2003.[1]

In fact, the Libyan decision is best understood in the broader context of the Bush Administration's determination to take effective action — including the use of force, if necessary — to counter the growing threat from proliferation. This determination, evident from the beginning of the President's first term in office, was reflected in: (1) the articulation of the first national comprehensive strategy to combat WMD; (2) the successful non- and counterproliferation initiatives championed by the Administration, including interdiction; and (3) the innovative use of intelligence and other national and multilateral tools to disrupt and defeat WMD proliferation threats from hostile states and non-state proliferation networks.

## *Articulating the Strategy*

At the outset of his first term, President Bush identified the proliferation of weapons of mass destruction and their possession by rogue states or terrorists as the preeminent threat to American security, and declared that countering these threats would be his top national security priority. By making clear the nature of the terrorist enemy, and especially its objective of killing large numbers of Americans, the September 11 attacks on the U.S. homeland made combating the spread of WMD even more urgent. Well before those attacks however, the President had outlined the need to develop new concepts and new capabilities to counter today's threats, rather than those of the Cold War.

The President and his top advisors understood from the start that successful protection against the full range of WMD threats would require fundamental change in how the United States and other countries perceive and respond to the proliferation challenge. Traditional nonproliferation measures, while essential, were not sufficient to prevent, and did little to protect against, this complex set of threats. Within the U.S. Government, this meant that the United States would no longer simply react to proliferation after the fact with political condemnations and, as appropriate, economic and other sanctions. Instead, there was a recognition that the United States must actively work to prevent proliferation and roll it back. Regarding other governments, Washington would need to convince friends and allies that proliferation is a matter of highest priority for them as well. Regarding proliferators, the United States would seek to send a strong message to countries like Libya: no longer could they proceed apace with their WMD and missile programs untroubled by potential consequences.

In his first speeches on national security policy, the President emphasized that, in a little over a decade, the security environment had changed fundamentally from a world in which the foremost challenge to U.S. security came from one centrally-controlled, bureaucratically-bound state, with defined borders and known leaders, to one in which outlaw regimes or shadowy groups of non-state actors were secretly attempting to buy, build, or steal the means to produce and use weapons of mass destruction. While the United States no longer was threatened by an adversary armed with thousands of nuclear weapons on a high state of alert, the prospects for the use of WMD against U.S. forces and the American homeland had possibly increased. This was a result of the changed nature of the threats faced by the United States: hostile regimes such as North Korea and Iran which sought WMD and long-range missiles for blackmail, and terrorists who perceived WMD as weapons of choice to maximize the number of American deaths they could inflict.

Consistent with these changes, the President immediately began to establish a new conceptual framework to combat today's WMD and missile threats, putting in place a comprehensive strategy involving proactive diplomacy, actions to counter proliferation directly, and better means for organizing and equipping the United States and its friends and allies to respond to the use of such weapons. The message was clear to all: the United States was serious in its determination to prevent and protect against these threats, and would use all of its tools — diplomatic, economic, scientific and technological, and military — to achieve this goal.

At the National Defense University in May 2001, the President outlined the urgent need to think and act differently to combat post-Cold War threats, especially those from WMD proliferation. (Full text at Annex A.) While this speech at the time was mischaracterized by some as having a single focus on missile defense — which, according to Administration critics, reflected a fixation with ending the 1972 ABM Treaty — it was, in fact, much broader. It included a call to take advantage of new opportunities, such as building a positive cooperative relationship with Russia, and a call to develop new capabilities and concepts of operation to dissuade, deter, and defend against WMD proliferation.

The President stated: "Today's world requires a new policy, a broad strategy of nonproliferation, counterproliferation and defenses."[2] While the President did call for ending the ABM Treaty and for the deployment of missile defenses against a North Korean-type threat, he made it clear that this capability was only one of many needed to deter and defeat the emerging chemical, biological, and nuclear threats to the United States and its allies. High-level teams were dispatched to Europe and Asia to consult with friends and allies on missile defense, as well as the underlying changes in the security environment and the President's strategic vision for counter-ing WMD threats more broadly. These consultations were highly visible — covered extensively in the European and Asian press in a way that could not escape the attention of Libya and other WMD proliferators.

A second milestone in the development of the U.S. strategy to combat WMD was the publication in September 2002 of the National Security Strategy, a document that reflected the impact of the September 11 attacks on the United States. Confronted by a terrorist enemy that would seek to kill as many Americans as possible, it was now even more urgent to prevent adversaries from threatening the United States and its allies with WMD. The document outlined the Administration's WMD strategy, including:

- Proactive counterproliferation efforts such as detection, active and passive defenses, and counterforce capabilities to protect against the threat.
- Strengthened nonproliferation efforts to prevent rogue states and terrorists from acquiring the means necessary for weapons of mass destruction.
- Effective responses to limit the casualties and damage if WMD is used against U.S. forces or population.[3]

The strategy was built on the premise that traditional concepts of deterrence are ineffective against an enemy whose avowed tactics are wanton destruction and the targeting of civilians. Thus, in an age when America's enemies openly seek the world's most destructive technologies, the United States cannot remain idle as dangers emerge. This is not a strategy of preemption, although the preemptive use of force is reaffirmed as an available option under certain conditions, especially given the possible catastrophic consequences of the use of WMD. Rather, it is a strategy to deal with the full spectrum of WMD threats and the full range of capabilities to counter these threats.

In December 2002, the Administration published the National Strategy to Combat Weapons of Mass Destruction. (Full text at Annex B.) Acknowledging directly the great diversity in WMD threats — that Iran is different from North Korea, Syria is different from Libya, and the terrorist WMD challenge is different from state threats — the document provided greater detail on the three pillars initially presented in the National Security Strategy:

- Protection or counterproliferation, including interdiction, deterrence, and defense;
- Prevention or nonproliferation, including support for accords such as the NPT, CWC, and BWC, increased non-proliferation assistance, greater controls on nuclear materials and exports and increased sanctions; and,
- Improved capabilities for response or WMD consequence management.[4]

To integrate the pillars, the strategy called for improvements in several key enabling functions, including: intelligence collection and analysis, research and development, international cooperation, and targeted strategies against state and non-state proliferators.

Promulgated publicly at the time the United States was leading the international effort within and outside of the UN Security Council to compel Iraq to account for its WMD programs and activities, the National Strategy to Combat Weapons of Mass Destruction received substantial attention in the U.S. and foreign press. While coverage of these events differed from paper to paper and country to country, one theme was constant: the United States would no longer tolerate the continued proliferation of WMD and missiles by states it considered threats. The impact of this coverage on the Libyan leadership would become evident.

## *Promoting Effective International Initiatives*

To implement the national strategy, the President initiated an active, highly-visible, diplomatic campaign to encourage other states to join in the effort to prevent and protect against WMD proliferation. In the G-8 meeting hosted in Kananaskis, Canada, in the summer of 2002, he successfully proposed the establishment of the Global Partnership Against the Proliferation of Weapons and Materials of Mass Destruction, with the goal of providing $20 billion over 10 years for Nunn-Lugar type threat reduction and nonproliferation projects, initially focused in Russia. Ten billion dollars was to come from the United States, with a matching contribution from the other G-8 partners and other states that chose to contribute.

In May 2003, the President announced a second, highly-visible initiative that drew worldwide attention. Made public at a press conference in Krakow, Poland, the Proliferation Security Initiative (PSI) would create a coalition of the willing to disrupt the trade in proliferation-related materials and equipment through proactive enforcement of national and international authorities. The success of the Initiative came early: in the highly-publicized Statement of Interdiction Principles committing participants to take effective action against proliferation transactions; in the conduct of operational exercises around the globe — at sea, on land and in the air — and, in the rapidly expanding list of countries to express support. (By mid-2008, over 90 countries have endorsed the Initiative — by any standard an unparalleled speed for gaining international participation.) Within the PSI framework, the United States also was able to sign landmark ship-boarding agreements with Panama, Liberia, and the Bahamas — the world's three largest commercial vessel registries — and concluded similar agreements with other nations.

The approach to PSI differed from that employed in most nonproliferation initiatives which seek universal membership even at the cost of accepting a negotiated, least common denominator outcome. With PSI, the effort started with a small (albeit geographically diverse) group. This group set the bar high in terms of the commitments participants would need to make. Having done so, participation was then opened up for others based on a voluntary willingness to meet those commitments. The immediate value of this novel approach to proliferation later would be seen in the interdiction of a ship carrying thousands of centrifuge parts to Libya for its nuclear weapons program.

In the counterproliferation field, a number of initiatives to develop improved capabilities for deterrence and defense against WMD threats also received wide attention in the international press. Missile defense was a key priority to bolster deterrence and protection against states such as North Korea and Iran. The U.S. withdrawal from the ABM Treaty and the President's public announcement that the United States would deploy a defense of all 50 states against a North Korean-type ballistic missile attack made headlines in the world press. No one questioned whether the President would to do whatever was necessary to protect the United States from WMD threats.

Another much-publicized priority was adapting U.S. nuclear forces to the new security environment, as reflected in the Administration's 2001 Nuclear Posture Review. The NPR specifically updated U.S. strategic planning to help address the new threats posed by proliferation. Administration briefings and unauthorized leaks of the findings and recommendations of the Review were covered extensively in the international media. A May 2003 report carried in the Libyan press, noted:

A dozen years after the Cold War's close raised hopes for an end to the nuclear threat, the Bush Administration is embarking on a quest for a new generation of nuclear bombs that are smaller, less powerful — and that the Pentagon might actually use in battle. In its nuclear posture review of 2001, the Administration urged development of a wide range of new nuclear capabilities, and said the U.S. might, in some circumstances use nuclear weapons against countries that do not have them: Syria, Libya, Iran and Iraq.[5]

Despite its inaccuracies, this and other similar reports in the Libyan press undoubtedly registered with Colonel Qadaffi and the Libyan leadership.

The United States also took visible steps to prepare for, and defend against, chemical and biological attacks. The Defense Department's acceleration of biological detection and medical protection capabilities, including the vaccination of forces against smallpox and anthrax, received significant attention in the world press. Also widely covered was the Administration's establishment of the domestic Bioshield program to accelerate the development and procurement of new medicines to treat victims of biological attacks.

As with the public articulation of a comprehensive strategy to combat WMD, implementing effective multilateral initiatives such as PSI and acquiring new capabilities to deter and defend against WMD showed clearly the seriousness with which the Bush Administration pursued the goal of combating WMD and missile proliferation. The President was direct in stating publicly his determination to stop the trade in proliferation and to develop counterproliferation capabilities needed to deter and defend against WMD threats from hostile states and terrorists. His announcement of the Proliferation Security Initiative in Poland emphasized these points to the world audience:

The greatest threat to peace is the spread of nuclear, chemical, and biological weapons. And we must work together to stop proliferation. ...When weapons of mass destruction or their components are in transit, we must have the means and authority to seize them. So today I announce a new effort to fight proliferation called the Proliferation Security Initiative. The United States and a number of our close allies, including Poland, have begun working on new arrangements to search planes and ships carrying suspect cargo and to seize illegal weapons or missile technologies. Over time, we will extend this partnership as broadly as possible to keep the world's most destructive weapons away from our shores and out of the hands of our common enemies.[6]

In this way, while increasing our national efforts to prevent proliferation in the first instance, the President added a new dimension to combat weapons of mass destruction and their means of delivery. Interdiction would block proliferation directly and produce incontrovertible evidence of its attempt. The threat of the use of force to defend U.S. security meant that those who illicitly pursued these weapons must consider carefully the risks inherent in their actions. Both of these factors would impact directly the Libyan decision to abandon WMD and longer-range missiles.

## Disrupting and Defeating WMD Threats

Libya initially asked to meet with U.S. and UK officials to "clear the air" about WMD programs in Libya only days before the invasion of Iraq in March 2003. That invasion followed more than six months of intense, and highly visible, diplomatic maneuvering at the UN in New York and in the Middle East and Gulf region. President Bush and Prime Minister Blair were the leading advocates of the effort to compel Saddam to account for the chemical, biological, and nuclear materials and activities that remained obscured by more than a decade of Iraqi denial and deception. There was general agreement that Iraq's actions constituted material breach of numerous Security Council resolutions going back more than a decade. The President and Prime Minister showed they were determined to enforce these resolutions and hold Iraq accountable on WMD, even if force was required. The U.S. and UK position was clear: Saddam needed to make a strategic choice — either he could choose to cooperate fully with international inspectors and provide a complete and accurate accounting of Iraq's programs, or he would be removed from power.

The buildup of hundreds of thousands of U.S., UK and other coalition troops sent a tough message not only to Baghdad, but also to others who sought WMD, especially in the region. Words — that those who seek such weapons will put their security at risk — were being backed by action. In Libya, which had long possessed chemical weapons and had embarked on a large-scale effort to be able to enrich uranium for nuclear weapons, the message was clearly received. The immediate concern of the Libyan leadership was that, after Iraq, it would be the next target for U.S. military action. This concern may well have been aggravated in the late fall of 2002 by stories in the international press, sourced to Israeli Prime Minister Sharon, that Iraq had sent a number of its nuclear physicists to Libya to work on a joint nuclear weapons program.

The Libyan press, a reflection of the regime's interests, took a strong early position against the "aggression" against an Arab "brother country." In October 2002, government-sponsored street demonstrations in Tripoli protested "the continuing insults to the Arab nation" by the "American threats to launch an aggression against the Iraqi people." Libya went as far as threatening to leave the Arab Union because of Qadaffi's assessment that other Arab states were not standing up to the American forced disarmament of Iraq.[7]

The reaction of declared "outrage" would be repeated consistently over the next several months. Libyan television reporting on March 20, 2003, described the government-supported street demonstrations in Tripoli as the "rejection of the American-British aggression against the Iraqi people" and "marches of raging anger and indignation." In parallel, Libyan diplomacy, including a public push for resolutions by Arab League Foreign Ministers and the UN Security Council, emphasized the international legal imperative of respecting the sovereignty of Iraq and its leadership.[8]

Two prominent themes in the Libyan-supported media appeared designed to build a "united Arab defense" against this growing concern by Colonel Qadaffi's regime that it would be next. The first theme was the effort to associate the "aggression" in Iraq with aggression against the entire Arab world: "This brutal war on Iraq... is a war on the entire Arab existence. It is a war, first of all, on the Arab dignity, and second, it is a war aimed at changing the map of the Arab world."[9]    In this regard, the Libyan press repeatedly described the conflict in Iraq as a "colonialist project to control the land, geography, and cancel Arab history, nationalism, culture and will." Here, two motives — oil and Zionism — were ascribed to the West: "It is greedy colonialism that rushes to usurp Iraq's oil and wealth and to kill the seeds of progress, nationalism, dignity and Arabism in its heroic people." The "plan" to destroy Iraq was termed a "U.S.-Zionist plan" intended to destroy "the whole of the Arab existence."[10]

The second theme was a renewed call for Arab unity in standing up to the expanding threat from the United States and its allies. If the conflict could be portrayed as a conflict against all Arabs, then all Arab governments needed to act forcefully to prevent any further aggression. For its part, Tripoli revived the dormant project of union among Libya, Egypt and Sudan. In May, a Libyan paper called for the "embryonic project" for this "trilateral union" to be "hastenly [sic] activated" with the goal of setting "the right foundation for a wider Arab union conducive to Arab's greater unity." It argued: "Regional and international circumstances and events in Palestine and Iraq prompt activation of the pan-Arab project if Arabs really wanted to live in peace and secure the future of the next generations."[11]

A number of factors appeared to converge in early 2003 that may have aggravated Tripoli's concern that, after Iraq, Libya would be next. One ostensible indicator was Washington's stepped-up campaign in January to deny Libya the chairmanship of the UN Commission on Human Rights. Another indicator may have been press stories out of Washington that U.S. intelligence believed Libya, which it described as a state sponsor of terror, was expanding its nuclear infrastructure and pursuing chemical and biological weapons capabilities. Together, these and other U.S. actions in the region suggested to the Libyan leadership that the United States would seek "regime change" in Libya. Little doubt exists that this concern was real and served as a motivation for Colonel Qadaffi to reach out to the United States.

Qadaffi sought accommodation on two key issues of central importance to the United States. First, in a January 2003 interview with *Newsweek*, he stressed that support in the Arab world for Osama bin Laden was a threat not just to the United States but also to his own rule. Noting that he was a target of an al-Qaeda assassination attempt, he indicated that Libyan intelligence would cooperate to "wipe out" this threat through the exchange of information with the United States and Great Britain.[12] Second, in March 2003, Qadaffi embarked on a secret initiative, approaching the United States through British intelligence contacts for a dialogue on WMD. While intimating that "everything would be on the table" and that Libya would be willing to renounce WMD, absent from the Libyan request was any formal acknowledgment of a nuclear program or any commitment to abandon it. In fact, Tripoli continued to deny publicly that such a program existed; for example, Libya publicly rejected claims by U.S. intelligence that it was seeking weapons of mass destruction. In January 2003, Libyan Foreign Ministry spokesperson, Hassouna al-Shawesh, emphasizing that Libya was a signatory of the Nuclear Non-Proliferation Treaty, dismissed a U.S. charge that it was building its nuclear infrastructure: "These are allegations the CIA habitually puts out to serve interests hostile to the peoples" of other states.[13]

Given Libya's public posture, the March 2003 request to "clear the air" on WMD was more likely an attempt to hedge against what Tripoli saw as a potential liability to the regime than a signal of intent to abandon WMD programs. At that time, fear of regime change was uppermost. On the eve of the coalition invasion of Iraq, Qadaffi stated in an interview with a French newspaper: "Once Bush has finished with Iraq, we will very soon be targeted."[14]

# III. Libya's Motivations

A number of apparent motivations were in play as the Libyan leadership worked through the decision to end their WMD and longer-range missile programs. A desire to lift economic sanctions, an interest in engaging more broadly with the West, and the presence of U.S. and coalition forces in the Middle East were major motivations for the Libyans to renounce and dismantle their WMD programs. The interdiction of the *BBC China* apparently also played an essential role in the outcome. Moreover, lengthy discussions with senior Libyans revealed additional underlying motivations, including combating Islamic extremism and concern for the legacy of the Qadaffi regime.

## *Desire to Lift U.S. Sanctions*

Relations between the United States and Libya broke down soon after the 1969 coup that overthrew the monarchy and brought Colonel Qadaffi to power. In particular, Libyan support for, and involvement in, international terrorism resulted in the withdrawal of the U.S. Ambassador from Tripoli in 1972, the closing of the U.S. embassy in 1981, and the concomitant expulsion of Libyan diplomatic personnel in Washington. During the next decade, Libya was involved in a number of terrorist acts — including the murder of a British police officer in 1984, the bombing of a Berlin discotheque in 1986, and the bombing of Pan Am 103 in 1988 and the French UTA flight in 1989 — and provided support throughout this period for the Abu Nidal terrorist group.

As a consequence of its terrorist activities, the costs to Libya grew. In 1979, the United States declared Libya to be a state sponsor of terror. In January 1986, President Reagan imposed sanctions on Libya under the International Emergency Economic Powers Act and the 1985 International Security and Development Act. These sanctions, expanded over time through Executive Order and additional legislation, banned almost all forms of economic trade between Libya and the United States.  The sanctions provided for broad prohibitions on direct and indirect aid and on imports from and exports to Libya — including the import of oil and the supply of oil production and refining equipment.  U.S. sanctions also were extended to ban travel to Libya, to prohibit credits and loans, as well as to bar U.S. contracts with foreign companies which invested in the Libyan oil sector.

In 1991, two Libyan intelligence agents were indicted in the United States and Scotland for involvement in Pan Am 103.  In January 1992, the UN Security Council passed Resolution 731 which demanded the surrender of the Libyan suspects, cooperation with the ongoing Pan Am and UTA investigations, payment of compensation to the families of the Pan Am victims, and cessation of all Libyan support to terrorism.  In March 1992, the Security Council imposed sanctions on Libya for its refusal to comply.  In November 1993, the Security Council adopted Resolution 883, providing for a limited freeze on Libyan assets and an embargo on selected oil equipment.

The economic and other costs to Libya from U.S. and UN sanctions would have an important impact on Libyan motivations.  As a consequence, Libya took substantial actions to meet the demands made by the United Nations, the United States, and other governments.  In 1999, Libya paid compensation for the killing of a British policewoman, a move that led to the re-opening of embassies in London and Tripoli.  Also in 1999, the Libyan government ended the presence of the Abu Nidal group on its territory and paid compensation to the families of the victims of the UTA flight.  Finally, again in 1999, Tripoli surrendered two individuals suspected of participation in the Pan Am bombing.  As a result, UN sanctions were lifted in September 2003, after Tripoli met all UNSC requirements — including official acknowledgement of responsibility for the Pan Am 103 bombing and payment of compensation to the families.

In response to Libya's acceptance of responsibility for Pan Am 103 and its financial settlement with the families, the Bush Administration notified the Security Council in August 2003 that it "would not oppose" the lifting of sanctions.  However, the official U.S. statement went on to emphasize:

> We remain deeply concerned about other aspects of Libya's behavior, including its poor human rights record

and lack of democratic institutions; its destructive role in perpetuating regional conflicts in Africa; and, most troubling, its pursuit of weapons of mass destruction and their related delivery systems. Libya also remains on the state sponsors of terrorism list, which carries its own sanctions.[15]

A second U.S. statement noted: "The United States will intensify its efforts to end threatening elements of Libya's behavior, and U.S. bi-lateral sanctions on Libya will remain in full force until Libya addresses these concerns."[16]

In sum, by the summer of 2003, Libya had acted to meet the demands made by the UN Security Council. Clearly, Tripoli was seeking to end all international sanctions against it — sanctions that were extracting a high price on the country's economy, including its ability to explore for, produce, and sell oil. While the lifting of UN sanctions was important to Libya, U.S. sanctions continued in force. Tripoli now knew that it would need to address the other concerns identified by the United States before it could expect relief from these sanctions.

One principal concern was the pursuit of WMD and longer-range missiles. In early 2003, however, the Libyan government remained far from even an acknowledgement of possessing such weapons programs, and even further from a commitment to eliminate them. While this would change over the course of the year, the motives for this change were far more complex than the desire to end U.S. sanctions.

## *Fear of Attack*

Libya's investment in its WMD and missile programs was substantial — in terms of financial resources, the involvement of many civilian and military personnel, and the lingering perception that such capabilities contributed to national security and prestige. When Libya initially approached the United States through the United Kingdom in March 2003, as coalition forces were being deployed to compel Iraq to comply with its UNSC obligations on WMD, Tripoli was most likely acting to hedge its position on WMD programs;  it had not yet made the strategic decision to abandon them.

As noted, the timing of the Libyan approach to the United States and the United Kingdom was more than coincidental.  The show of U.S. and UK resolve in Iraq encouraged the perception that WMD proliferation carried a high risk to the regime. In fact, Colonel Qadaffi reportedly explained to congressional delegations in January and March 2004 that, "one of the reasons... he was giving up the weapons [of mass destruction] was he did not want to be a Saddam Hussein, and he did not want his people to be subjected to the military efforts that were being put forth in Iraq."[17] Italian Prime Minister Berlusconi would quote Qadaffi a few months after the invasion as saying: "I will do whatever the United States wants, because I saw what happened in Iraq, and I was afraid."[18]

## *Exposure and Disruption of the Nuclear Program*

Another factor that played a major part in Libya's decision to end its long-standing and expensive investment in WMD and longer-range missiles was the penetration and unraveling of the A.Q. Khan proliferation network.  These two intelligence successes — convincing and compelling Libya to end its WMD programs, and the takedown of the Khan network — intersected at a number of key points.  The operations against the network provided critical evidence about the Libyan nuclear program that was instrumental in persuading Tripoli to abandon its efforts; and furthermore, evidence acquired on the ground in Libya about the network proved a fatal blow to Khan and his associates.

Upon entering office, the Bush Administration was presented with a still-emerging picture of a major illicit network which spanned three continents and sold sensitive nuclear technologies to countries like North Korea, Iran, and Libya.  Beginning in the 1990s, U.S. and UK intelligence services had worked in close partnership to learn about the operations of the network.  After 2001, the focus would shift to taking it down.

Mr. Khan, the "father" of Pakistan's nuclear weapons program, over the course of three decades had put together a close group of partners who provided sensitive materials to Pakistan's effort. At some point, Khan decided to branch out and set up a new business to support a lavish lifestyle, including ownership of a luxury hotel in Timbuktu. As more and more information was gathered on the network, the key nodes of the operation became known, including the central clearing-house and shipment point in the United Arab Emirates (UAE) under the management of B.S.A. Tahir, who acted as the network's Chief Executive Officer. Tahir, under Khan's direction, loosely managed the network's many procurement and production agents in the Netherlands, Germany, Switzerland, Turkey and South Africa. Tahir also directly oversaw the network's manufacturing facility in Malaysia which produced many essential parts for centrifuge cascades.

As more information was gathered about the many components of the Khan operation, opportunities were created to penetrate its activities clandestinely. In the fall of 2003, this penetration would produce actionable intelligence on a major shipment of centrifuge parts manufactured at the network facility in Malaysia and shipped through Dubai to Libya. Departing aboard a German-owned vessel, *BBC China*, from the UAE in late September 2003, the shipment provided an early test of the PSI and a critical opportunity to disrupt the Libyan nuclear weapons program through interdiction. When first approached, Berlin and Rome immediately agreed to assist in the operation — both citing their status as core members of the recently-established PSI. After observing the *BBC China's* movement from Dubai through the Suez Canal, U.S. and UK intelligence officers worked with the German and Italian governments to divert the ship in early October to a port in Italy where five large containers of centrifuge parts were unloaded.

The evidence from the *BBC China*, once shown to the Libyans, would have an immediate effect. Tripoli may well have concluded that its nuclear program — dependent on the Khan network — was now vulnerable to further disruptions and increased costs. It also may have thought that, now exposed, the program was even more likely to be the target of a U.S. attack. Given these apparent motivations, Libya quickly agreed on a specific date for the long-standing request to permit U.S. and UK experts to visit Libya, and to provide those experts with access to facilities and individuals involved in the WMD and missile programs.

With this agreement, and perhaps without a full understanding of its consequences, Libya had moved yet another step closer to a strategic decision to abandon its WMD programs. Once in country, U.S. and UK experts would compile evidence revealing the presence of chemical, nuclear, and longer-range missile programs. CIA Director George Tenet later would testify on the success of the expert teams:

> [During] nine months of delicate negotiations... we moved the Libyans from a stated willingness to renounce WMD to an explicit and public commitment to expose and dismantle their WMD programs. The leverage was intelligence. Our picture of Libya's WMD programs allowed CIA officers and their British colleagues to press the Libyans on the right questions, to expose inconsistencies, and to convince them that holding back was counterproductive. We repeatedly surprised them with the depth of our knowledge. For example, US and British intelligence officers secretly traveled to Libya and asked to inspect Libya's ballistic missile programs. Libyan officials at first failed to declare key facilities, but our intelligence convinced them to disclose several dozen facilities, including their deployed Scud B sites and their secret North Korean-assisted Scud C production line.[19]

## *Combating Islamic Extremism*

For several years, the Libyans waged their own conflict with Islamic extremists — mostly the Libyan Islamic Fighting Group (LIFG) — who had sworn to destroy the Qadaffi regime. Having observed the U.S. reaction to September 11, the war in Afghanistan, and the preparation for war in Iraq, the Libyans believed that only the United States was strong enough and determined enough to strike back against Islamic terrorism. The Libyans believed they needed to align themselves with the United States against Islamic extremism because they were no longer sure they could defeat their extremist enemy alone.

## *Search for a New Legacy*

Based on comments by senior Libyans, it also appeared that Libyan leaders, including Colonel Qadaffi and members of his inner circle, had begun to assess their legacy and were disturbed by what they saw. Isolation from the West had not worked, as Libyan society was stunted in its economic and educational growth. The journey through pan-Arabism and pan-Africanism had not been keys to development, and the impending removal of Saddam Hussein only highlighted the fragility of dictatorial, isolated governments. WMD programs had not provided Libya with the additional strength and stature that could help overcome all of the other shortcomings. Consequently, it became obvious to some clear-thinking senior Libyans that these programs needed to be ended in order to move the society forward.

A net assessment of Libyan perceptions and motivations suggests heightened costs in the continued pursuit of WMD, lowered value in the acquisition of these weapons, and sharp risks in continued hostility toward the United States. U.S. and UK commitments to improved relations following Libyan abandonment of WMD and longer-range missiles represented considerable value for Colonel Qadaffi, especially under this set of circumstances.

# IV. Libya's Weapons Programs

Upon entering office, the Bush Administration received intelligence assessments of Libyan WMD and missile programs that, while observing Tripoli's continuing interest in acquiring WMD and more capable ballistic missiles, did not indicate programs of the same scale or urgency as those of North Korea and Iran. The "Unclassified Report to Congress on the Acquisition of Technology Relating to Weapons of Mass Destruction and Advanced Conventional Munitions, 1 January Through 30 June 2001" provided the following characterization:

> Libya is continuing its efforts to obtain ballistic missile-related equipment, materials, technology, and expertise from foreign sources. Outside assistance — particularly Serbian, Indian, North Korean and Chinese — is critical to its ballistic missile development programs, and the suspension of UN sanctions in 1999 has allowed Tripoli to expand its procurement effort. Libya's current capability probably remains limited to its SCUD B missiles, but with continued foreign assistance it will probably achieve an medium-range ballistic missile (MRBM) capability — a long-desired goal — or extended-range Scud capability.
>
> Libya remains heavily dependent on foreign suppliers for precursor chemicals and other key CW-related equipment. Following the suspension of UN sanctions in April 1999, Tripoli reestablished contacts with sources of expertise, parts, and precursor chemicals abroad, primarily in Western Europe. Libya still appears to have a goal of establishing an offensive CW capability and an indigenous production capability for weapons. Evidence suggests Libya also is seeking to acquire the capability to develop and produce BW agents.

Libya — an NPT party with full scope IAEA safeguards —continues to develop its nuclear research and development program but would still require significant foreign assistance to advance a nuclear weapons option. The suspension of UN sanctions has accelerated the pace of procurement efforts in Libya's drive to rejuvenate its ostensibly civilian nuclear program. In January and November 2000, for example, Tripoli and Moscow renewed talks on cooperation at the Tajura Nuclear Research Center and discussed a potential power reactor deal. Should such civil-sector work come to fruition, Libya could gain opportunities to pursue technologies that could be diverted for military purposes.

Following the suspension of UN sanctions, Libya has negotiated — and completed — contracts with Russian firms for conventional weapons, munitions, and upgrades and refurbishment for its existing inventory of Soviet-era weapons.[20]

One year later, the assessment appeared little changed in terms of the scale and urgency of the Libyan programs. The "Unclassified Report to Congress on the Acquisition of Technology Relating to Weapons of Mass Destruction and Advanced Conventional Munitions, 1 January Through 30 June 2002" reads:

*Nuclear.* An NPT party with full-scope IAEA safeguards, Libya continued to develop its nuclear infrastructure. The suspension of UN sanctions provided Libya the means to enhance its nuclear infrastructure through foreign cooperation and procurement efforts. Tripoli and Moscow continued talks on cooperation at the Tajura Nuclear Research Center and a potential power reactor deal. Such civil-sector work could present Libya with opportunities to pursue technologies that also would be suitable for military purposes. In addition, Libya participated in various technical exchanges through which it could try to obtain dual-use equipment and technology that could enhance its overall technical capabilities in the nuclear area.  In 2001, Libya and other countries reportedly used their secret services to try to obtain technical information on the development of WMD, including nuclear weapons.  Although Libya made political overtures to the West in an attempt to strengthen relations, Libya's continued interest in nuclear weapons and nuclear infrastructure upgrades raises concerns.

*Missile.* The suspension of UN sanctions in 1999 allowed Libya to expand its efforts to obtain ballistic missile-related equipment, materials, technology, and expertise from foreign sources.  Outside assistance — particularly from Serbian, Indian, Iranian, North Korean, and Chinese entities — has remained critical to its ballistic missile development programs.  Libya's capability is improving and with continued foreign assistance it will probably achieve an MRBM capability — a long-desired goal — or extended-range Scud capability.

*Chemical and Biological.*  Libya also remained heavily dependent on foreign suppliers for CW precursor chemicals and other key related equipment.  Following the suspension of UN sanctions, Tripoli reestablished contacts with sources of expertise, parts, and precursor chemicals abroad, primarily in Western Europe.  Tripoli still appeared to be working toward an offensive CW capability and eventual indigenous production.  Evidence suggested that Libya also is seeking to acquire the capability to develop and produce BW agents.[21]

A close reading makes evident two significant changes from the 2001 report. First, in the missile area, the report suggested Libya was now closer to its goal of acquiring an extended range SCUD capability. Second, the report expressed increased concern about the nuclear program.  Two sentences are of particular note: "In 2001, Libya and other countries reportedly used their secret services to try to obtain technical information on the development of WMD, including nuclear weapons. Although Libya made political overtures to the West in an attempt to strengthen relations, Libya's continued interest in nuclear weapons and nuclear infrastructure upgrades raises concerns." This new information reflected the intelligence that was now being acquired from the penetration of the A.Q. Khan nuclear proliferation network, specifically the large-scale involvement of that network in the Libyan covert centrifuge program.

A year later, the "Unclassified Report to Congress on the Acquisition of Technology Relating to Weapons of Mass Destruction and Advanced Conventional Munitions, 1 January Through 30 June 2003" continued to express growing concerns on the nuclear and missile fronts:

> *Nuclear.* An NPT party with full-scope IAEA safeguards, Libya continued to develop its nuclear infrastructure. The suspension of UN sanctions provided Libya the means to enhance its nuclear infrastructure through foreign cooperation and procurement efforts. Tripoli and Moscow continued talks on cooperation at the Tajura Nuclear Research Center and a potential power reactor deal. Such civil-sector work could have presented Libya with opportunities to pursue technologies also suitable for military purposes. In addition, Libya participated in various technical exchanges through which it could have tried to obtain dual-use equipment and technology that could have enhanced its overall technical capabilities in the nuclear area. Although Libya made political overtures to the West in an attempt to strengthen relations, Libya's assertion that Arabs have the right to nuclear weapons in light of Israel and its nuclear program — as Qadhafi stated in a televised speech in March 2002, for example — and Tripoli's continued interest in nuclear weapons and nuclear infrastructure upgrades raised concerns.

> *Ballistic Missile.* The suspension of UN sanctions

in 1999 allowed Libya to expand its efforts to obtain ballistic missile-related equipment, materials, technology, and expertise from foreign sources. During the first half of 2003, Libya continued to depend on foreign assistance —particularly from Serbian, Indian, Iranian, North Korean, and Chinese entities — for its ballistic missile development programs. Libya's capability therefore may not still be limited to its Soviet-origin SCUD B missiles. With continued foreign assistance, Libya will likely achieve an MRBM capability — a long-desired goal — probably through direct purchase from North Korea or Iran.

*Chemical and Biological.* Libya also remained heavily dependent on foreign suppliers for CW precursor chemicals and other key related equipment. Following the suspension of UN sanctions, Tripoli reestablished contacts with sources of expertise, parts, and precursor chemicals abroad, primarily in Western Europe. Libya has indicated — as evidenced by its observer status at the April 2003 Chemical Weapons Convention Review Conference and previous Convention Conferences of States Parties — a willingness to accede to the CWC. Such efforts are consistent with steps that Tripoli is taking to improve its international standing. Tripoli still appeared to be working toward an offensive CW capability and eventual indigenous production. Evidence suggested that Libya also sought dual-use capabilities that could be used to develop and produce BW agents.[22]

The new concern with Libya was most directly reflected in the prepared remarks for the "DCI's Worldwide Threat Briefing" on February 11, 2003. In that testimony, CIA Director Tenet placed the Libyan programs in the broader context of the rise of new, non-state suppliers and of the breakdown of the traditional nonproliferation regimes:

More has changed on nuclear proliferation over the past year than on any other issue. For 60 years, weapon-design information and technologies for producing fissile material — the key hurdles for nuclear weapons production — have been the domain of only a few states. These states, through a variety of self-regulating and treaty based regimes, generally limited the spread of these data and technologies.

In my view, we have entered a new world of proliferation. In the vanguard of this new world are knowledgeable non-state purveyors of WMD materials and technology. Such non-state outlets are increasingly capable of providing technology and equipment that previously could only be supplied by countries with established capabilities.

This is taking place side by side with the continued weakening of the international nonproliferation consensus. Control regimes like the Non-Proliferation Treaty are being battered by developments such as North Korea's withdrawal from the NPT and its open repudiation of other agreements.

The example of new nuclear states that seem able to deter threats from more powerful states, simply by brandishing nuclear weaponry, will resonate deeply among other countries that want to enter the nuclear weapons club.

Demand creates the market. The desire for nuclear weapons is on the upsurge. Additional countries may decide to seek nuclear weapons as it becomes clear their neighbors and regional rivals are already doing so. The "domino theory" of the 21st century may well be nuclear.

With the assistance of proliferators, a potentially wider range of countries may be able to develop nuclear weapons by "leapfrogging" the incremental pace of weapons programs in other countries.

Mr. Chairman, I want to mention our renewed concern over Libya's interest in WMD. Since the suspension of sanctions against Libya in 1999, Tripoli has been able to increase its access to dual-use nuclear technologies. Qadhafi stated in an *Al-Jazirah* interview last year that Arabs have "the right" to possess weapons of mass destruction because, he alleges, Israel has them.

Libya clearly intends to reestablish its offensive chemical weapons capability and has produced at least 100 tons of chemical agents at its Rabta facility, which ostensibly reopened as a pharmaceutical plant in 1995.[23]

While the above assessments reflected a growing concern with Libyan WMD and missile programs, the actual size and scale of these programs became clear only after the visits of U.S. and UK experts to Libyan WMD and missile facilities in October and December 2003. The greatest effort was in the nuclear weapons program, in which the Libyans had invested an estimated $100 to $200 million over a number of years, and was far more advanced than earlier assessments had suggested. What would soon be catalogued and removed from Libya was astounding, ranging from weapons design documentation to thousands of parts for the sophisticated P2 centrifuge. While it would have taken substantial time and effort for Libya to produce a nuclear weapon, the revised intelligence assessment was that Libya was well on its way to developing a nuclear weapons capability.

Some observers, particularly those closely associated with the IAEA, which sought initially to downplay the size and advanced status of the Libyan program, noted that Libya possessed only a small number of P2 rotors and had only a start-up quantity of UF6 feed material. These individuals, however, often failed to acknowledge that Tripoli possessed the specialized equipment and materials for P2 rotor production and was working on obtaining a domestic production capability for UF6. In fact, Libya already had tested some centrifuges and had placed an order for parts for up to 10,000 machines, sufficient to produce enough fissile material for multiple weapons each year. Moreover, Tripoli already had acquired nuclear weapons design documents from the Khan network.

Having been caught once again totally unaware of a covert nuclear weapons program being conducted by an NPT party, the initial IAEA response predictably was defensive. In early January 2004, Dr. Mohamed ElBaradei, Director General of the IAEA, described the Libyan nuclear program as "low level, small scale testing of enrichment equipment" that consisted of "nothing really special... mothballed and in containers." Moreover, the IAEA Director General appeared reluctant to characterize the existence of weapons design information and hundreds of tons of undeclared nuclear equipment as evidence of a "weapons" program — even after the explicit acknowledgement of a weapons program by the Libyan government. Equally predictable and defensive, the Director General asserted to the press that "we have the mandate and we intend to do it [presumably the investigation] alone." The IAEA also downplayed the Libyan decision and emphasized that the "nascent" Libyan program was "years from developing nuclear weapons." But the facts spoke to the Libyan commitment to develop a nuclear weapon and the true status of the program. Within several months, after gathering the facts and conducting inspections of facilities that had not been previously known to, or visited by, IAEA personnel, the Agency's line would change substantially.[24]

In addition to the nuclear weapons program, U.S. and UK inspectors on the ground in October and December 2003 learned the details of the Libyan chemical and ballistic missile programs. The chemical program included approximately 25 tons of mustard agent produced about ten years before and located at a number of less-than-fully-secured sites, as well as over 3,000 unfilled munitions. It also included the equipment to begin a second production line for more advanced agents, as well as precursors that could be used to produce mustard and nerve agents.

Libya also provided U.S. and UK teams with extensive documentation and other information on its SCUD missile force, its program to develop longer-range missiles, and its assistance from North Korea, Iran, and other sources. Libya's missile inventory included six extended-range SCUD C missiles, complete with erector launchers and control equipment, and over 400 SCUD B missiles with a range of approximately 300 kilometers.[25]

Finally, the Libyans acknowledged a past intention to develop biological capabilities, but it was not evident whether this was for defensive or offensive purposes. U.S. and UK experts were given access to Libyan biological experts at a number of dual-use facilities, including a number of civilian medical, biotechnical, and agricultural research centers.

# V. The Timeline

On December 19, 2003, Colonel Qadaffi announced that Libya voluntarily had decided to give up its nuclear and chemical weapons programs and longer-range missiles, making clear that he now believed that these weapons programs no longer added to Libya's security or well-being. In March 2004, the ship, *Industrial Challenger*, arrived in the United States with over 500 metric tons of cargo — including everything from centrifuges to Libya's 800 km range SCUD C force. This marked an end to Tripoli's nuclear weapons program and its possession of longer-range missiles, one of the most significant nonproliferation achievements to date.

It is useful to recognize a number of key milestones between Libya's initial overture in March 2003 [26] and Qadaffi's strategic decision to abandon Libya's WMD and longer-range missile programs.

> **April 2003**: The first meeting is held among U.S., UK and Libyan intelligence personnel during which there is discussion of the need for a technical visit to Libya by U.S. and UK experts. No agreements are reached. Musa Kusa, head of Libyan intelligence, is the principal Libyan interlocutor, and remains so throughout the process.

> **August 2003**: Agreement is reached within intelligence channels to meet with Colonel Qadaffi to discuss the prospect for a technical visit.

> **September 2003**: U.S. and UK intelligence officials meet in Tripoli with Colonel Qadaffi during which he agrees in principle to allow the technical visits, but defers to his senior leadership to work out the details. No date for the technical visit is agreed upon during the follow-on discussions.

> **October 3, 2003**: Interdiction of the ship, *BBC China*, occurs

en route to Libya: five large 40-foot shipping containers marked "used machine parts" are offloaded in an Italian port and are determined to contain thousands of centrifuge parts manufactured in Malaysia by the A.Q. Khan nuclear proliferation network.

**October 7, 2003**: Evidence of a nuclear program is presented to the Libyans; Libya immediately agrees on dates for a visit of the U.S./UK technical team.

**October 19-29, 2003**: Technical team conducts first on-site visit.

**November 2003**: Trilateral meeting is held following the completion of the first technical visit. The Libyans are presented with additional intelligence concerning their nuclear program. Arrangements are agreed upon for a second technical visit.

**December 1-12, 2003**: U.S./UK technical team conducts second on-site visit.

During the first visit of the technical team, much was learned about Libya's WMD and missile programs. By the end of the second visit, the Libyans:

- Admitted having a nuclear weapons program and having bought uranium hexafluoride feed material for gas centrifuge enrichment.
- Acknowledged having made about 25 tons of sulfur mustard chemical weapons agent, aerial bombs for the mustard, and small amounts of nerve agent.
- Agreed to inspections by the IAEA and the OPCW, and to abide by the range limitations of the MTCR.

Perhaps most encouraging, as well as most disturbing, at the end of the second visit the Libyans handed over nuclear weapons design materials to the U.S. and UK experts — documentation acquired from A.Q. Khan that possessed an alarming level of detail, identifying everything Libya would need to make a nuclear bomb. This revelation would set the stage for the policy meeting.

While a number of questions remained even after the return of the experts in December — including the precise nature of the North Korean connection to Libya's missile project, the extent of work on nerve agents, and the possibility of hidden centrifuges — the intelligence assessment was that sufficient confidence existed to proceed to policy discussions and that these outstanding questions should not be an obstacle to moving forward. In fact, the assessment was that the best means of addressing outstanding issues was to continue and deepen the engagement with Libya (by both U.S. and UK experts, as well as through the OPCW and IAEA), thereby allowing for further access to Libyan personnel and facilities.

# VI. The End Game

The first policy discussion with the Libyans was held in seclusion in London on December 16, 2003. Prior to that session, at the final meeting of the second technical visit in country, Libya had agreed to make a public statement that would: (1) admit to having chemical and nuclear weapons programs; (2) commit to accept intrusive inspections and monitoring from the IAEA and OPCW; (3) commit to eliminate CW stocks and munitions and its nuclear weapons program; and (4) commit to adhere to standards set by the MTCR. Colonel Qadaffi had not approved any official statement nor had he agreed to make a statement under his own name, although his representatives thought he would want to make it as a personal statement because "if he made it, the President would then respond and this would help to overcome skeptics within the Administration." While the Libyans did not provide a copy of a draft statement during the technical team's visit, they did agree to provide a text before the policy meeting. They failed to do so.

**Tuesday, 16 December**

The initial opening statement by the Libyan side moved backwards from the commitments made just days before the London meeting. In fact, the very first remarks from the Libyan participants focused on the need to remove sanctions. The response from the U.S. and UK representatives was that the focus must be on a public acknowledgement of Libya's WMD programs and on Tripoli's commitment to abandon its nuclear, chemical, and longer-range ballistic missile capabilities.

U.S. and UK officials made clear that the purpose of the meeting was not to negotiate specific steps or responses to Libyan actions on the part of the United States and United Kingdom. They stated that, if Libya did move forward with its commitment to end its WMD and longer-range missile programs, one major barrier to improved relations would be removed.

The draft opening statement on WMD proposed by the Libyan side emphasized the need to rid the world of WMD and suggested that the Libyan statement was being offered as a gesture at Christmas. Most significant, the text failed to mention the existence of Libyan WMD programs or make a commitment to eliminate them. It read:

> In view of the international climate that prevailed during the Cold War, as well as the tension and imbalance of power among its countries through which the Middle East was facing, the Jamahiriyah, along with some countries of the region, called for making the Middle East region and Africa a WMD free zone. This call did not receive a serious response from all the region's countries. And out of the Jamahiriyah's belief that an arms race is a programme that does not serve neither the security of Libya nor the security of the region it also contradicts with its great keenness for world peace and security.

> At a time when the world is celebrating the birth of Jesus — may peace be upon Him — and as a contribution for obtaining a world full of peace, security, stability and compassion, the great Jamahiriyah decided to keep only defensive weapons that are in conformity with agreed standard (criteria) set out by the MTCR in a clear way that can be verified. The Jamahiriyah also confirms its full commitment to the Nuclear Non-Proliferation Treaty and its respect (adherence) to the IAEA Convention. The Jamahiriyah concluded the International Treaty on the Ban, Producing, Storing and Use of Chemical Weapons (CW). This treaty was ratified in accordance with Iam No. (18) of the year 1371 of the d.p. corresponding to 2003 of the B.J. All the necessary measures for implementation are under way. The Jamahiriyah is also about to set up a national corporation with the aim to secure contacts with the organization on

chemical weapons ban, it further pledges its commitment to additional protocols to these conventions.

Whilst the Great Jamahiriyah has conducted constructive talks with the U.S.A. and U.K. on W.M.D. programmes, it renews its honest call to make the Middle East Region together with Africa a W.M.D. free zone.

Frank and intense discussion went on for almost six hours on the need for the Libyan statement to acknowledge WMD programs and provide an unambiguous commitment to abandon these programs.

The discussion of the text of the Libyan statement was followed by an even more tense discussion of what actions Libya would need to take in order to eliminate its WMD and longer-range missile programs. The U.S. representative raised the requirement for an explicit commitment from the Libyan delegation to eliminate WMD and longer-range missile programs. The initial response of the Libyan delegation was that "the position of the Libyan government is known." When told that this response was insufficient, the second response was that U.S. and UK intelligence officers knew the Libyan position. Again stating that the Libyan reply was insufficient, the U.S. representative emphasized the need for explicit agreement at the table from the Libyan representatives to the following commitments:

*Nuclear:* (1) removal of all materials and equipment related to the nuclear weapons programs: all centrifuges and all parts and associated equipment; all UF6 and other nuclear materials; all UCF equipment; all documentation; (2) implementation of the Additional Protocol.

*Chemical:* (1) elimination and destruction of all chemical agents, munitions, and equipment; (2) complete accession to the Chemical Weapons Convention.

*Biological:* (1) complete openness and allow monitoring

of facilities; (2) formal commitment not to pursue BW
capabilities.

*Missiles:* (1) removal of all ballistic missiles
with a range greater than 300 km (SCUD Cs)
as well as all associated equipment; (2) no
development or deployment of ballistic missiles with
a range greater than 300 km; (3) adherence to the
parameters of the MTCR.

U.S. and UK representatives stressed that Libyan agreement
to these precise commitments was essential if there was to be
a successful conclusion to the talks. As a consequence, the
Libyan participants agreed to each point, as well as to the
requirement for international monitoring and inspections in all
WMD and missile areas.

While all of the above commitments were important,
two were unique and precedent-setting. The first was the removal
of all components of the nuclear program. This was essential for
avoiding a future problem should the Libyans later argue that
equipment acquired for activities such as uranium conversion or
even enrichment could be retained for a "peaceful" nuclear
program.  The Iran case, of cynically manipulating the provisions
of the NPT to acquire sensitive technologies for weapons
purposes under the guise of a peaceful program, was very
much present in the minds of the U.S. and UK participants.
Confirming that this was a real possibility, Saif al-Islam stated
publicly on December 20, one day after the announcement of
the Libyan decision: "Of course, this program could be used for
peaceful purposes."[27] However, by this time, the commitment to
remove all such equipment had been obtained. The second
unique and precedent-setting commitment was the elimination
of missile capabilities beyond a 300 km range.

For their part, the Libyan participants emphasized the
importance of characterizing their decision to abandon WMD and
longer-range missiles as "voluntary" and in Libya's self-interest.
U.S. and UK representatives were quick to agree that this was
accurate and should be done.

**Wednesday, 17 December**

U.S. and Libyan participants returned to their respective capitals.

**Thursday, 18 December**

When the meeting on December 16 ended, it was unclear how Colonel Qadaffi would react to the draft statement hammered out at the table. To encourage Libyan acceptance of the statement, and to get final buy-in from Qadaffi, Prime Minister Blair reached out to the Libyan leader. In an unprecedented conversation between these two men, lasting almost thirty minutes, Colonel Qadaffi reportedly was concerned about: (1) the appearance of the Libyan decision being portrayed as caving in to pressure, and (2) the prospect that Libya would be attacked because it had now admitted that it possessed WMD programs. Qadaffi was concerned about the wording of the text and stated that he would have his Foreign Minister make the formal announcement. The Prime Minister gave assurances that a Libyan statement — if clear on possession and elimination — would be met with positive statements by the United States and United Kingdom.[28]

In a discussion following the call with Colonel Qadaffi, President Bush and Prime Minister Blair reportedly exchanged views on next steps. There was complete agreement that the language of the Libyan announcement must be clear as to the existence of WMD programs and the commitment to abandon them, and that Colonel Qadaffi must make it known that he personally authorized the statement. Both also agreed that U.S. and UK responses to an acceptable Libyan announcement would make it evident that there would be positive consequences if Libya ended its WMD programs.

Following these two conversations, Libyan officials provided two alternative drafts of a statement by the Libyan Secretary of the General Popular Committee for External Relations (Libyan Foreign Minister). They informed the United States and United Kingdom that, if either one of the two versions was acceptable, Tripoli would broadcast it on Friday. They also noted that, if Washington and London could not agree to either text, Libya would be content to have Washington and London announce the decision and Tripoli would not deny it. The two texts read:

**VERSION A**

Draft announcement issuing from the Great Socialist Popular Libyan Arab Jamahiriyah:

In view of the international climate that prevailed during the Cold War, as well as the tension within the Middle East region, the Jamahiriyah, along with some other countries in the region, called for making the Middle East and Africa a WMD free zone. Because this call did not receive a positive response from all of the countries in the region, and after Libya had confirmed, as the world knows, that those who hold Libya to be an enemy, themselves possess WMD, Libya decided, out of self defence in accordance with Article 51 of the UN charter, to develop its defensive capabilities.

In view of the end of the Cold War and the emergence of an intention and determination across the world to get rid of WMD in all their forms, especially after the spreading of the phenomenon of revolt and uncontrolled terrorism and the fear of the transfer of these weapons into the hands of irresponsible persons which could amount to a threat against everyone, and after work with nuclear states with permanent seats on the UNSC and responsible for international security and peace, Libya, of it own free will, decided to limit itself to conventional defensive weapons in accordance with the prescriptions of MTCR and Libya will adopt these steps with verifiable transparency. Libya also confirms and will abide by its commitments under the NPT, its IAEA Safeguards Agreement and the Biological Weapons Convention including the Additional Protocol and the BWC.

Libya's belief is that an arms race does not serve its security nor the security of the region, but conflicts with Libya's great concern for a world blessed with security and peace. We hope that this work will be a model for others to follow.

At a time when the world is celebrating the birth of Jesus, the Great Jamahiriyah renews its sincere call for a WMD free zone in the Middle East and Africa.

**VERSION B**

Draft announcement issuing from the Great Socialist Popular Libyan Arab Jamahiriyah:

In view of the international climate that prevailed during the Cold War, as well as the tension within the Middle East region, the Jamahiriyah, along with some other countries in the region, called for making the Middle East and Africa a WMD free zone. Because this call did not receive a positive response from all of the countries in the region, Libya decided to develop its capabilities in addition to long-range missiles.

Libyan experts have worked during the past months with experts from the nuclear states which are permanent members of the UNSC responsible for international peace and security.

As a result, of its own free will, Libya has decided to abandon these programmes with the aim of completely eliminating WMD in all the states of the Middle East region and Africa, and to limit its rockets to the ranges agreed in the MTCR regime.

Libya will take these steps with verifiable transparency. Libya also confirms that it will abide by the NPT and by the safeguards agreements of the IAEA and the BWC including the additional protocol of the IAEA and the BWC.

Libya's belief is that an arms race does not serve its security nor the security of the region, but conflicts with Libya's great concern for a world blessed with security and peace. Libya's desire of this initiative is that all states will follow Libya's model, beginning with the Middle East region without exception at all.

**Friday, 19 December**

Neither of the two versions from December 18 was considered sufficiently precise in acknowledging WMD programs and making a clear commitment to eliminate them.  Through the UK channel in Tripoli, Washington and London provided inputs to the language that would address these deficiencies.  Yet another draft was received from Libya in mid-afternoon Washington time.  This version came close to what was required.  A final brief exchange produced agreement on what all three sides could accept, including references to centrifuge and chemical weapons programs, and an explicit obligation for immediate international inspections, including monitoring of Libya's missile force to meet its commitment not to develop and deploy capabilities beyond a 300 km range.

During the next several hours, U.S. and UK officials were in constant contact awaiting confirmation of the Libyan statements. During this time, the Libyans sent word to Washington and London that Qadaffi's statement would be released as a written statement. Although a last-minute change from what had been expected to be an in-person announcement, this was considered acceptable — perceived as a face-saving step by Qadaffi.

The tense wait went well into the afternoon Washington time, late evening in London.  Finally, confirmation was received that the Libyan statements had been made.  The statement made by the Libyan Foreign Minister conformed to the agreed-upon text. The statement released in the name of Colonel Qadaffi was also sufficient to meet the requirements, explicitly referencing the abandonment of WMD programs.

Once the Libyan statements were confirmed, Prime Minister Blair and President Bush made their separate but coordinated announcements.  By agreement, the statement by the Prime Minister came first. Both emphasized the voluntary nature of Qadaffi's historic decision, the need for its quick, verifiable implementation, and the prospect for more positive relations with Libya in the future. (Full texts at Annex C.)

In a press background briefing immediately following the President's announcement, a senior official emphasized a number of themes in response to press questions: first, that the Libyan decision was a response to the "realistic" policies of the Bush Administration, especially the determination to make clear to proliferators that WMD do not bring prestige or security, but rather the contrary; second, that the Libyan experience creates a new model of cooperative disarmament that others should follow; third, while

Libya had been forthcoming in many areas and had provided considerable detail concerning its activities, a number of issues remained unresolved, requiring continued monitoring and verification; and fourth, there were no specific discussions about lifting sanctions or any other specific benefits; instead, the message was that, if Libya fulfills its commitments, there is a prospect for improved relations with the United States that will lead to benefits for the Libyan people. These themes and others were also included in a White House Fact Sheet. The text of the Fact Sheet reads:

> Libya has disclosed to the US and UK significant information on its nuclear and chemical weapons programs, as well as on its biological and ballistic missile-related activities, Libya has also pledged to:
>
> - Eliminate all elements of its chemical and nuclear weapons programs;
> - Declare all nuclear activities to the IAEA;
> - Eliminate ballistic missiles beyond 300 km range, with a payload of 500kg;
> - Accept international inspections to ensure Libya's complete adherence to the Nuclear Nonproliferation Treaty, and sign the Additional Protocol;
> - Eliminate all chemical weapons stocks and munitions, and accede to the Chemical Weapons Convention;
> - Allow immediate inspections and monitoring to verify all of these actions.
>
> As President Bush said today, Libya must also fully engage in the war against terror.
>
> Libya's announcement today is a product of the President's strategy which gives regimes a choice. They can choose to pursue WMD at great peril, cost and international isolation. Or they can choose to renounce these weapons, take steps to rejoin the international community, and have our help in creating a better future for their citizens.

These actions will make our country more safe and the world more peaceful.

There is no greater danger to our people than the nexus of terrorists and weapons of mass destruction. The risks posed by this dangerous nexus cannot be contained or deterred by traditional means. From the beginning of his Administration the President's national security strategy has committed the US to work with its allies to:

- Ensure that international agreements against the proliferation of WMD are observed and enforced;
- Detect, disrupt and block the spread of dangerous weapons and technology;
- Confront emerging threats from any person or state before those threats have fully materialized; and
- Improve our capabilities to respond to the use of WMD and minimize the consequences of an attack.

* * * *

Libya's announcement today is a product of this strategy. Over the last two years the world community has witnessed our determination to work in partnership with our allies to combat the nexus of terrorism and WMD. Together we have:

- Enforced UN Security Council resolutions to disarm the Iraqi regime;
- Removed the terrorist Taliban regime in Afghanistan;
- Expanded our intelligence capabilities, improved our technology, and increased allied cooperation;
- Captured or killed key terrorist leaders, disrupted and seized terrorist finances, and destroyed terrorist weapons and training camps;
- Led the Proliferation Security Initiative to interdict

dangerous WMD and their means of delivery.
- Continued our efforts to secure sensitive techno-logies in the former Soviet Union and elsewhere;
- Insisted on a multilateral approach to confront the threat from North Korea; and
- Supported the work of the International Atomic Energy Agency to hold the Iranian regime to its treaty obligations.

These actions have sent an unmistakable message to regimes that seek or possess WMD: these weapons do not bring influence or prestige — they only bring isolation and other unwelcome consequences. When leaders make the wise and reasonable choice to renounce terror and WMD, they serve the interests of their own people and add to the security of all nations.

Another message should be equally clear: leaders who abandon the pursuit of chemical, biological and nuclear weapons — and the means to deliver them — will find an open path to better relations with the US and other free nations.

Other leaders should find a constructive example in Libya's announcement. Genuine progress by Libya to eliminate its WMD programs will be met by tangible improvements in relations with the world community.

The US and UK have a troubled history with Libya, and serious issues remain. However, Libya has taken a significant step, and with this decision Libya has begun the process of rejoining the international community. As Libya becomes a more peaceful nation, it can be a source of stability in Africa and the Middle East.[29]

# VII. Implementation: The "Outing" of WMD

Although the December public announcements made visible the U.S./UK/Libya trilateral process, all three parties sought to conduct the follow-on discussion on implementation in private. All, therefore, maintained a low profile in public statements and presence. The U.S. representation to the second policy discussion, held in London on January 5, 2004, was identical to that of December 19, with the addition of a notetaker from the Department of State. The UK and Libyan teams were also similar, if not identical, in composition.

The political atmosphere for the January meeting was starkly different from that of December. The emphasis of all three sides was on cooperation and getting the job of disarmament done expeditiously and in partnership. All three delegations stressed the progress made in the three weeks since the December 19 meeting.

U.S. and UK participants made the following points during the discussion:

- Libya's decision to pursue cooperative disarmament of its WMD programs was well received around the world. This decision served as a positive example for other states to follow. The President was clear when he said, "leaders who abandon the pursuit of chemical, biological, and nuclear weapons and the means to deliver them, will find an open path to better relations with the United States and other free nations. ...Libya has begun the process of rejoining the community of nations." It is of mutual interest to complete the process of verifiable disarmament as quickly as possible.
- The United States and United Kingdom look forward to working with Libya in a spirit of cooperation and partnership to implement the Libyan commitments in the nuclear, chemical, biological, and missile areas.
- To get the process underway, the United States and

United Kingdom request sending a small team to Libya
as early as the week of January 12.  The purpose of
the team would be to: (1) assist in preparation of
declarations; (2) begin removal of sensitive nuclear
components and documents; (3) conduct discussions
on the Additional Protocol; and (4) begin implementation
of Libya's chemical weapons, biological weapons, and
missile commitments.

- The United States and United Kingdom are willing to
explore the prospect of funding the elimination of these
programs.  Both also are willing to consider assistance
in retraining and employing Libyan personnel to limit the
possibility of proliferation, as has been done in former
Soviet states.  To give assistance, it would be essential
that Libya agree to provide full liability protections and
immunities.
- The U.S. and UK effort would operate concurrently with,
and be mutually supportive of, that of the OPCW in the
chemical area and the IAEA in the nuclear area.

On nuclear elimination, U.S. and UK officials made the following
points:

- When in country, the joint team would inspect and
secure the containers in which Libya's Highly Enriched
Uranium (HEU) is stored.  First priority would be given
to removing immediately the materials and documentation that are the most sensitive from a proliferation
perspective.  These would include all warhead-related
documents and all HEU.
- If the HEU containers are in satisfactory condition,
the team would work with their Libyan counterparts
to prepare and load the containers for shipment out
of Libya.  If the containers are damaged or corroded,
the sides would need to work together to repackage
the HEU.  Permission would be needed to use military
aircraft to land in Libya to remove the HEU.
- Regarding other nuclear weapons-related components,

Libya should permit the U.S./UK team to visit any location where Libya has conducted work on the design, development, testing, or production of a nuclear weapon or any components.

- Libya should work to begin removing as soon as practical all UF6, all centrifuges and critical centrifuge components, while ensuring that all such sensitive equipment is effectively secured in Libya until such time as it can be removed. After that, all uranium conversion equipment, natural uranium, and equipment for manufacturing centrifuges would be removed.

- Finally, regarding assistance in the nuclear area, Libya should begin implementation of its commitment to adhere to the Additional Protocol and to apply the Protocol provisionally pending its entry into force. The U.S., UK and Libyan experts should also begin to discuss assisting Libya in preparing its Additional Protocol and other IAEA declarations.

On chemical weapons, the U.S. and UK representatives emphasized a number of actions Libya should accomplish in cooperation with the United States and United Kingdom:

- While Libya had completed all legal measures necessary to accede to the CWC, it could not legally become a party to the Convention until it deposited its instrument of accession. The Libyan government should present an instrument of accession to the Secretary General of the United Nations in New York, as soon as possible.

- Once Libya becomes a Party to the CWC, there will be a number of declarations that Libya will need to submit to the OPCW in The Hague. These declarations can be complicated, but U.S. and UK experts have substantial experience with such matters, and would assist Libya in preparing them.

- Libyan CW stocks are a potential target for terrorists, as well as a potential environmental hazard. It would serve Libyan interests, as well as those of the rest of the world, to ensure physical security around those storage sites as rapidly as possible. U.S., UK and Libyan experts should discuss possible security enhancements.

- In previous statements, Libya listed a number of munitions that were designed to be filled with chemical agents. These munitions ought to be destroyed as soon as possible. Since they do not contain chemical agents, this should be a relatively simple physical task.
- Libya should begin and complete destruction of its chemical munitions and agent stockpiles quickly and in accordance with the CWC. The United States and the United Kingdom would like to work with Libya on how to achieve this, including assistance with developing destruction plans for approval by the OPCW.

On biological activities, the U.S. and UK representatives welcomed the Libyan commitment not to pursue a biological weapons program and to comply fully with the BWC, and noted:

- The United States and United Kingdom accept the Libyan pledge to allow inspections and monitoring of its biological activities. The trilateral experts should consider how best to achieve this goal.
- It is in Libya's interest to establish strong security and accountability practices to ensure that there is no danger of biotechnology facilities, equipment, or materials being diverted to illicit purposes.
- The United States and United Kingdom are working hard domestically to improve their own security practices, as agreed to at the November 2003 meeting of States Parties to the BWC. U.S. and UK experts could assist Libya in developing security measures and programs which Libya could put in place. Having such security programs would make Libya's facilities much more attractive to foreign firms — who are unlikely to invest in dual-use industries if uncertain whether they are properly secured.

On missiles, the U.S. and UK representatives welcomed the Libyan decision to eliminate, and not to develop in the future, all missiles with a range greater than the standard set in the Missile Technology Control Regime, making the following points:

- The MTCR standards cover all rocket systems and all unmanned air vehicle (UAV) systems capable of delivering a payload of at least 500 kilograms to a range of at least 300 kilometers.
- Trilateral experts need to discuss the MTCR and the related conventions, and their implications for the implementation of Libya's pledge. These experts should verify the elimination of certain systems, including the SCUD B and C missiles and related equipment.
- Libya's commitment to eliminate MTCR-class missiles includes the following actions: (1) elimination of all MTCR-class missiles; (2) not resuming the development, testing, production, deployment or acquisition/possession of MTCR-class rocket or UAV systems; and (3) not to assist other countries in any way in the development or acquisition of WMD-capable delivery systems, including application of export controls called for in the MTCR Guidelines and Annex.

Throughout the session, all three sides emphasized that the spirit was one of cooperation and partnership. The Libyan representatives agreed to all U.S./UK proposals regarding the site visits and approaches to implementation. The Libyan side was particularly attracted to the offer of assistance in the retraining of scientists, viewing this as a means to have Libyan students once again enroll in American universities. Most importantly from their perspective, the Libyans stressed again the need to characterize the Libyan decision as "voluntary" and to approach all issues on a basis of partnership with the United States and United Kingdom, as well as with the OPCW and IAEA.

In an aside with the head U.S. representative, one Libyan official remarked that he now understood why the U.S. side had been so insistent on gaining specific and explicit commitments from the Libyan delegation at the December policy meeting, especially that all nuclear equipment be removed and that all chemical weapons and longer-range missiles be eliminated. He said that he now understood the usefulness of insisting on a clear commitment in this regard and that, because there was no longer any ambiguity about Libya's commitments, many internal disputes had been settled by this prior agreement.

When the U.S. and UK experts arrived in Libya on January 12, 2004, the positive results of the U.S./UK insistence on clarity and transparency immediately became apparent. The head of the U.S. team, Ambassador Donald Mahley, described the "atmospherics" as follows:

> Much has been written about the need for the United Nations Special Commission (UNSCOM) personnel to be good interrogators with bulldog tenacity to extract from an unwilling Iraqi host the information and even the access sought. But the Libyan decision had been communicated downward through the Libyan government. When we asked to go to a location, we were taken there. When we asked to see equipment, or inside buildings, or a site where we thought there might be some activity that had not been declared, we got what we asked for, in the overwhelming majority of cases quickly and with outstanding effort on the part of our Libyan hosts.[30]

The positive results of this cooperative effort could be seen immediately. Beginning on January 23, and continuing through March 6, 2004, the United States removed from Libya the following nuclear materials, as documented by the Department of Energy:

- 1.8 metric tons of UF6 (5-10 MT of natural UF6 could produce enough HEU for a weapon.) The HEU associated with Libya's research reactor was subsequently repackaged and removed.
- A modular uranium conversion facility, which could produce Uranium Dioxide (UO2), UF4, or uranium metal (Libya also sought, but did not receive, complementary equipment to produce 15-30 tons of UF6 a year).

- 20 complete P1 centrifuges and most of the components for an additional 200 P1 centrifuges.
- Two P2 (advanced) test centrifuges, and thousands of parts under an order for 10,000 P2 centrifuges. (10,000 P2 centrifuges could produce enough HEU for about 10 nuclear weapons a year.)
- Nuclear weapons design information.
- Two flow-forming machines and 35,000 kg of maraging steel to make P2 rotors.

Over 3,000 unfilled chemical munitions were destroyed under U.S. supervision within the first few months of the year. Moreover, the stockpiles of CW agents were quickly consolidated, and security measures greatly improved pending final elimination. On January 14, 2004, The Hague announced that, "Libya had filed necessary paper-work with United Nations and will formally become the 159th country to join Chemical Weapons Convention on 5 February." Just how far Libya had moved in a few short months was evident in a statement by the Director General of the OPCW in March 2004: "I think they were pretty close to producing nerve gases."[31]

On missiles, the Libyans agreed to the early removal of the SCUD Cs, as well as the transporter-erector-launchers (TELs) and other supporting equipment. One of the first steps taken was to remove the guidance sets for these missiles, which were flown out on January 27, along with the other most sensitive materials, including stock to enrich uranium and sensitive centrifuge parts. The missiles themselves were shipped out in March to the United States.

Yet another precedent-setting commitment would also be fulfilled within a few months. On May 13, 2004, the Libyan government made the following announcement:

> As part of its efforts to strengthen peace and stability in the world, in the context of which Libya announced in December 2003 that it renounced programs, materials and equipment which might lead to the production of internationally banned weapons or delivery systems, as classified by the MTCR, Libya wishes to announce officially the application of this decision to its military dealings with other states. Libya will not deal in any

military goods or services with states which Libya considers to be of serious weapons of mass destruction proliferation concern.[32]

In a press interview later that day, Under Secretary of State John Bolton elaborated:

We have discussed this question expressly with the Libyans and do have an understanding of what it covers. And that's why this is a particularly important announcement because the Government of Libya has assured the United States and the United Kingdom that its renunciation of all military trade with states of serious WMD proliferation concern includes North Korea, Syria and Iran.[33]

The scale of the success with Libya would be put in perspective in July 2004 during the visit of President Bush to the Oak Ridge National Laboratory, the site at which most of the Libyan nuclear equipment was stored. In his remarks, the President emphasized the importance of the success in getting Libya to abandon its WMD and longer range missile programs: (Full text at Annex D.)

...I've just had a close look at some of the dangerous equipment secured in this place. Eight months ago, the centrifuge parts and processing equipment for uranium were 5,000 miles away in the nation of Libya. They were part of a secret nuclear weapons program. Today, Libya, America and the world are better off because these components are safely in your care.

These materials are the sobering evidence of a great danger. Certain regimes, often with ties to terrorist groups, seek the ultimate weapons as a shortcut to influence. These materials, voluntarily turned over by the Libyan government, are also encouraging evidence that nations can abandon those ambitions and choose a better way.

Libya is dismantling its weapons of mass destruction and long-range missile programs. This progress came about through quiet diplomacy between America, Britain and the Libyan government. This progress was set in motion, however, by policies declared in public to all the world. The United States, Great Britain, and many other nations are determined to expose the threats of terrorism and proliferation — and to oppose those threats with all our power. We have sent this message in the strongest diplomatic terms, and we have acted where action was required.

Every potential adversary now knows that terrorism and proliferation carry serious consequences, and that the wise course is to abandon those pursuits. By choosing that course, the Libyan government is serving the interests of its own people and adding to the security of all nations.

* * * *

Three years ago, the nation of Libya, a longtime supporter of terror, was spending millions to acquire chemical and nuclear weapons. Today, thousands of Libya's chemical munitions have been destroyed. And nuclear processing equipment that could ultimately have threatened the lives of hundreds of thousands is stored away right here in Oak Ridge, Tennessee. Today, because the Libyan government saw the seriousness of the civilized world, and correctly judged its own interests, the American people are safer.

Three years ago, a private weapons proliferation network was doing business around the world. This network, operated by the Pakistani nuclear scientist, A. Q. Khan, was selling nuclear plans and equipment to the highest bidder, and found willing buyers in places like Libya, Iran, and North Korea. Today, the A. Q. Khan network is out of business. We have ended one of the most dangerous sources of proliferation in the world, and the American people are safer.

* * * *

All this progress has been achieved with the help of other responsible nations. The case of Libya's nuclear disarmament is a good example. In the fall of 2003, American and British intelligence were tracking a large shipment of nuclear equipment bound for Tripoli aboard a German-registered cargo ship. We alerted German and Italian authorities, who diverted the ship to an Italian port where the cargo was confiscated. We worked together. These events helped encourage Libya to reconsider its nuclear ambitions. That was a dramatic breakthrough, achieved by allies working together. And the cooperation of America's allies in the war on terror is very, very strong.

We're grateful to the more than 60 nations that are supporting the Proliferation Security Initiative to intercept illegal weapons and equipment by sea, land, and air. We're grateful to the more than 30 nations with forces serving in Iraq, and the nearly 40 nations with forces in Afghanistan. In the fight against terror, we've asked our allies to do hard things. They've risen to their responsibilities. We're proud to call them friends.[34]

# VIII. Lessons Learned

## *Demonstrate Seriousness*

From the outset of the Administration, the President emphasized the priority he placed on countering the proliferation of WMD and missiles, and his determination to combat this growing threat through all necessary means. His first major national security address in May 2001, four months before the September 11 terrorist attacks, not only identified WMD proliferation as a major threat to the United States, but made evident the need to adopt new strategies and develop new counterproliferation capabilities to meet this threat. This message was reinforced and magnified after September 11, as reflected in speeches at The Citadel and West Point.

The National Security Strategy and the National Strategy to Combat WMD, provided both the purpose and blueprint for action that the Administration would follow to prevent and protect against proliferation. The message was clear to all proliferators: the United States considered the spread of weapons of mass destruction and their possession by terrorists and rogue states to be a call for action. The nexus of proliferation and state sponsorship of terror, such as that found in Libya, was highlighted by the President as a particular concern.

In this context, the message to hostile states pursuing WMD and missile capabilities was serious and explicit: these weapons will not contribute to your security but will have the opposite effect. This message was clearly transmitted and, in the case of Libya, clearly received. The Libyan announcement on December 19, 2003, noted: "Libya's belief is that an arms race does not serve its security nor the security of the region, but conflicts with Libya's great concern for the world blessed with security and peace." Later, Colonel Qadaffi would make this point even more directly: "We made this step owing to a conviction of ours, that is because this programme is not useful to Libya, but it actually represents a danger and a threat to Libya's very integrity."[35]

## Insist on a Strategic Decision

At the time of the initial Libyan approach in March 2003 to "clear the air" on WMD, U.S. and UK officials were skeptical of Libyan motivations. Given the timing of the approach, it appeared likely that Libya's leadership was making a tactical move to hedge its position without acknowledging WMD programs or committing to their elimination.

Between March and October 2003, while the United States and United Kingdom remained skeptical, they made a sustained attempt to encourage the Libyans to be more forthcoming. But they viewed the reluctance of Libya to allow U.S. and UK experts into the country as an indication that the leadership had yet to make a strategic decision to abandon WMD capabilities. The U.S. and UK officials believed that only a strategic decision expressed by Colonel Qadaffi would produce the desired results by ensuring complete transparency into the history of the programs and full confidence in the elimination process.

While the interdiction of Libyan centrifuge parts in October 2003 led to agreement to permit U.S. and UK experts entry into the country, the Libyan leadership at the time of the first experts visit had still not made the necessary strategic decision. On the ground there was only an incremental opening of the Libyan programs to the U.S. and UK teams. By the end of the second visit in December, the Libyans had acknowledged the existence of chemical weapons and a nuclear weapons program, as well as a longer-range SCUD C force, and had indicated a willingness to eliminate these weapons and programs. But even then, more needed to be done.

It was not until the initial policy meeting on December 16, 2003, that Libya agreed explicitly to the requirement that it both publicly acknowledge the programs and commit to their elimination. Even at that meeting, the Libyan opening statement suggested Tripoli had actually moved backwards and would resist any reference in its public statement to the existence of actual programs or to their elimination.

Yet, the U.S. and UK participants believed that, without such a public acknowledgement and commitment, the strategic decision was absent. For this reason, U.S. and UK representatives pushed for this acknowledgement. Confidence that Libya had made the necessary strategic decision came only with the Libyan statement on December 19. Even then, President Bush's remarks made clear his intent to "trust but verify." The President stated that, while the Libyan decision was in itself a "development of great importance," it was still necessary for Tripoli to demonstrate "its seriousness" and "good faith" by meeting its commitment to complete and verifiable elimination of its WMD and longer-range missile programs.

The assessment that the Libyan leadership had not made the necessary strategic decision prior to the December 19 announcement was confirmed when the U.S. and UK teams arrived in country in January. The U.S. team leader would observe:

> Prior to the December 19 announcement, there had been dialogue and even visits by select U.S. and UK officials. However, Libya obviously had not made a truly authoritative "full disclosure" decision until it was so announced in December. When we arrived in January, we were voluntarily taken to additional resources that had not been discussed earlier. Our interlocutors were candid in advising us that they had not received instructions to be completely open earlier, so had only followed the instructions they had been given. The point here is not whether there was less-than-complete disclosure earlier, but to point out that the incomplete disclosures were coherent and internally consistent, and involved all the major facilities that would have been required for a complete program. The additional material disclosed in January would have taken a lengthy dialogue and on-site set of proced-ures to uncover without Libyan cooperation. The lesson to learn? It is relatively easy, even in a country where the bulk of the territory is open desert, to conceal elements of a WMD program if there is a national decision to do so. The idea that a single or even repeated short-time international inspection routine is sufficient to provide high confidence nothing has been missed is truly viewing the situation though rose colored glasses.[36]

## *Employ All Tools*

The Libyan experience demonstrates the requirement to bring into play all available tools to combat WMD proliferation — from diplomacy, to sanctions, to interdiction, to the use of intelligence and military force if required.    One essential tool, as noted, was the powerful message of resolve conveyed by the words and actions of the Administration.

The willingness to employ force against Iraq to enforce UN Security Council resolutions on WMD had a clear impact on the Libyan leadership.    One Libyan commentator noted on December 26, 2003: "I think that the climate that preceded and accompanied the war on Iraq has undoubtedly played a role in the Libyan decision."[37]    Despite assertions by Saif al-Islam that Tripoli did not "give into" the United States as a result of Iraq, there was real concern on Qadaffi's part that he would be next.[38]    In an earlier January 2004 interview, Saif stated:    "I was able to take messages to my father and explain to him [what was happening]. Once they assured us that they did not [secretly seek regime change], everything went forward."[39]

Another tool that clearly contributed to the Libyan decision was the interdiction, under the PSI, of centrifuge parts on the *BBC China*. Without the evidence provided by this interdiction, Libyan delay in permitting the visit of U.S. and UK experts would have almost certainly continued.    In turn, it was the knowledge of Libyan programs acquired by these teams that led to the full disclosure of the Libyan WMD and longer-range missile programs. And once disclosed, the prospective difficulties, costs, and risks of nuclear acquisition increased dramatically because the programs could no longer be conducted in secret. As a result, the pressure to agree to abandonment increased substantially.

An observation of the U.S. team leader based on his experience in Libya through March 2004 goes directly to this point:

> This [the interdiction of the *BBC China*] put a considerable crimp in both progress and the availability of replacement resources, not only from the cost involved but also from the perspective of making a supplier

more cautious for fear of having the entire network uncovered. It is clear that this event did not cause Libya to commence the quiet dialogue about the future of their WMD programs. However, it well could have accelerated their decision to renounce publicly all such activity.[40]

The President's public remarks on December 19 noted the importance of all the tools that were employed in achieving success with Libya:

> The United States and our allies are applying a broad and active strategy to address the challenges of proliferation, through diplomacy and through the decisive actions that are sometimes needed. We've enhanced our intelligence capabilities in order to trace dangerous weapons activities. We've organized a Proliferation Security Initiative to interdict dangerous materials and technologies in transit. We've insisted on multilateral approaches like that in North Korea to confront threats. We are supporting the work of the International Atomic Energy Agency to hold the Iranian regime to its treaty obligations.

> We obtained an additional United Nations Security Council Resolution requiring Saddam Hussein to prove that he had disarmed, and when that resolution was defied, we led a coalition to enforce it. All of these actions by the United States and our allies have sent an unmistakable message to regimes that seek or possess weapons of mass destruction. Those weapons do not bring influence or prestige. They bring isolation and otherwise unwelcome consequences.

The decision to use selected portions of clandestinely-collected intelligence to demonstrate to the Libyans the U.S./UK depth of knowledge of their WMD programs was also crucial in convincing the Libyans that the entire process had to be taken seriously. At times the Libyans were greatly disturbed by what they were told, but they appeared to develop significant respect for the U.S. and UK collection efforts, thereby enhancing the credibility of the U.S. and UK technical teams.

Uninformed, and almost always anti-Bush, critics consistently downplay the importance of the conflict in Iraq, the interdiction of the *BBC China*, and the use of intelligence in persuading Libya to abandon its WMD and longer-range missile programs.[41] Instead, while emphasizing the fact that a dialogue with Libya had begun before the war in Iraq, these critics stress the effect of sanctions and the utility of diplomacy in getting the Libyans to abandon these programs. This one-dimensional oversimplification not only distorts the actual events but risks failure of learning from this critically important experience. Sanctions were essential to the outcome. But without employing the other tools, the outcome would certainly have been different. In fact, it was by employing these additional instruments that diplomacy was empowered with greater effectiveness.

## *Create the Perception and Reality of a Win-Win Outcome*

Both the U.S. and UK sides were conscious from the beginning of the need to structure the outcome with Libya as a win-win: a nonproliferation victory for the United States and United Kingdom, as well as a political and national security victory for Libya. The first was easy; the second more difficult. The prevailing view was that, if Libya were to acknowledge and abandon these programs, it would be helpful if its leaders portrayed the outcome as contributing to Libya's own welfare and national security posture.

Moreover, the U.S. and UK participants understood that a win-win outcome would produce a second path, different from that of Iraq, for other would-be proliferators to follow — sending the powerful message that, if these countries also were to abandon their WMD programs, benefits would ensue. In the case of Libya, the United States and United Kingdom made clear that abandonment of these programs would remove a major obstacle to the improvement of relations. At the same time, the U.S. and UK participants emphasized that there were other impediments that needed to be addressed before the removal of sanctions and more normalized relations, especially Libyan support to terrorism.

In welcoming the Libyan decision, the President stated:

> As the Libyan government takes these essential steps and demonstrates its seriousness, its good faith will be returned. Libya can regain a secure and respected place among the nations, and over time, achieve far better relations with the United States. The Libyan people are heirs to an ancient and respected culture, and their country lies at the center of a vital region. As Libya becomes a more peaceful nation, it can be a source of stability in Africa and the Middle East.
>
> Should Libya pursue internal reform, America will be ready to help its people to build a more free and prosperous country... Because Libya has a troubled history with America and Britain, we will be vigilant in ensuring its government lives up to all its responsibilities. Yet, as we have found with other nations, old hostilities do not need to go on forever. And I hope that other leaders will find an example in Libya's announcement today.

The Prime Minister made a similar point:

> This courageous decision by Colonel Qadhafi is an historic one. I applaud it. It will make the region and the world more secure. It shows that problems of proliferation can, with good will, be tackled through discussion and engagement, to be followed up by the responsible international agencies. It demonstrates that countries can abandon programmes voluntarily and peacefully. The Libyan government has stated that weapons of mass destruction are not the answer for Libya's defence. No more are they the answers for the region. Libya's actions entitle it to rejoin the

> international community. I have spoken to Colonel
> Qadhafi to say that, as the process of dismantlement
> goes forward, I now look forward to developing a
> productive relationship with him and with Libya.

The President also emphasized the more general point that Libya
provides a new model for others to follow: "And another message
should be equally clear: leaders who abandon the pursuit of
chemical, biological and nuclear weapons, and the means to deliver
them, will find an open path to better relations with the United
States and other free nations." A similar point was included
in the Libyan statement: "Libya's desire of this initiative is that all
states will follow Libya's model, beginning with the Middle East
region without double standards."

The message of a second model was readily accepted and
promoted by the Libyan government. In early January, the editor of
the Libyan news agency emphasized that "with this bold decision,
the great Jamahiriyah has proved that it is the initiator and the
motivator of the countries of the world to get rid of the programs
and weapons of mass destruction, on the basis of its important and
leading role in building a new world free of these internationally
banned weapons and any kind of terrorism."[42] That the Libyan
decision had created a second model was also accepted by others in
the region. An early January 2004 article in Cairo's *Al-Ahram* notes:

> Washington seems to have offered the leaders of the
> region two models to choose from: The Iraqi model with
> its deposed president Saddam Husayn — he fought
> the U.S. power and refused to cooperate with it and
> ultimately ended up the way he did — and the Libyan
> model of eliminating banned weapons voluntarily,
> integrating Libya in the international community, and
> ultimately receiving rewards, both direct and indirect.[43]

Ensuring that Libya would benefit from taking the right course — and
thereby making clear to others that there was an alternative model
that they too could pursue to their benefit — became a priority for the
United States and United Kingdom. Within a year, Libya would begin
to gain substantially from its WMD decision as U.S. sanctions were

lifted and political relations with the United States were restored. By January 2005, a number of economic and political steps had been taken that, together, marked a profound positive change for Libya. In response to Libyan steps to eliminate their chemical, nuclear, and longer-range missile programs, the President lifted the national emergency imposed under the International Emergency Economic Powers Act, ended Executive Order sanctions, and terminated the applicability of the Iran-Libya Sanctions Act. These actions removed restrictions on travel, trade, and investment, and ended many disincentives for American companies interested in undertaking business ventures in Libya. Moreover, Libyan assets in the United States were "unfrozen" with over $1 billion being transferred back to Libyan ownership.

On the political front, a number of important steps also have been taken by the United States: direct diplomatic relations were re-established between Washington and Tripoli; the first meeting in 25 years took place between the Secretary of State and his Libyan counterpart; travel restrictions on Libyan diplomats in the United States were removed; and, exchanges were undertaken in the areas of health and education. The visits of Prime Minister Blair and others to Libya, including President Berlusconi, Spanish Prime Minister Aznar, and most recently Secretary Rice, also have demonstrated the value of Tripoli's actions to eliminate WMD and longer-range missile programs. Similarly, the invitation extended to Colonel Qadaffi for meetings with the European Union in Brussels, and the EU decision to lift its arms embargo, recognized the importance of Libya's abandonment of WMD capabilities.

## *Be Conscious of Face*

While firm and direct in their dealings with the Libyans in both intelligence and policy channels, U.S. and UK participants were very conscious that a Libyan decision to abandon WMD and longer-range missile programs would have to be voluntary, reflecting the strategic decision that such weapons were no longer in the nation's interest. While working to create the conditions for this outcome, including the interdiction of centrifuge components, they still recognized that a decision to end Libya's programs would be very difficult. These programs had cost Libya an estimated $100 to $200 million and involved the careers of many in Libya's military and scientific community. Giving them up would entail a degree of risk, even given the authoritarian nature of the regime. This perception of cost and risk can be seen in a public comment by Colonel Qadaffi: "If you declare you have a programme for building nuclear or chemical weapons, if you declare this before the entire world, well, this requires courage. Those who possess these weapons do not declare it, exactly because they do not have the courage."[44]

The capture of Saddam only three days before the December 19 policy meeting — and the images of the former dictator repeatedly flashed around the world — undoubtedly reinforced the conclusion of Libya's leaders that it was in their interest to abandon WMD programs. However, these images also made it even more important from Tripoli's perspective that the decision not be seen as yielding to U.S. pressure. All three sides shared the view that, if an agreement were perceived as a wholesale defeat for Colonel Qadaffi, the prospects for an agreement would be much reduced as Qadaffi's prestige would be undermined at home and in the broader Arab community. In sum, U.S. and UK participants understood the Libyan position and sought to accommodate it — while remaining firm in insisting on what Libya had to do to reach agreement.

Predictably, a number of opposition figures and a few governments, notably Iran and North Korea, criticized the Libyan decision as an act of capitulation to avoid the fate of Saddam.[45] However, this criticism received relatively little attention and had little noticeable impact. By speaking with a single voice emphasizing the voluntary nature of the decision, the United States, United Kingdom and Libya preempted those who would seek to use the decision for internal political purposes or those who would seek to deny the applicability of the model to their own WMD programs.

## *Ensure Direct Access to Leadership*

Another essential ingredient for success was direct access to, and the personal involvement of, the leaders of the three governments.

All three leaders considered the outcome a national security priority, and all were willing to invest their personal effort and accept the risk of failure. For the United States and United Kingdom, the President and Prime Minister remained intensely interested and closely involved throughout the course of the discussions. They were briefed frequently at each step by the intelligence officers interacting with the Libyans. They provided policy direction and, in so doing, made evident to all the importance they assigned to the outcome, and the requirement for secrecy. The President and Prime Minister were also willing to engage with Colonel Qadaffi, including by sending messages through the intelligence envoys.

Most obviously, Colonel Qadaffi's personal involvement was imperative to the outcome. In fact, as stated by the Libyan participants, only Qadaffi could make the strategic decision to acknowledge and abandon the Libyan WMD and longer-range missile programs. At each critical juncture, his advisors went to him for decisions which he made with caution and a degree of risk. It was clear from the Libyan participants that they would have preferred not to have taken to their leader the tough decisions that the U.S. and UK sides made necessary. They did so only because it was made clear to them that such decisions had to be made to accomplish their assigned task.

## *Ensure Complete and Continuing Access for Verification*

The Libyan experience makes evident once again that illicit activities by a state willing to cheat on its NPT and IAEA safeguard obligations are not likely to be detected by the international monitoring practices in place. IAEA inspections, based on visits to only a handful of declared sites, had provided the Agency with sufficient confidence to judge that there was no evidence that Libya was pursuing a nuclear weapons program. In fact, following Tripoli's strategic decision to abandon its weapons program, the Libyans provided U.S. and UK experts access to additional sites associated with its weapons program. The undeclared activities at these covert locations demonstrated that IAEA safeguards cannot uncover clandestine programs. While the Additional Protocol provides the Agency with more authority to pursue undeclared activities, it still must rely on the cooperation of the inspected state. The IAEA is not an intelligence organization. It lacks the authority and resources to undertake the mission of detecting covert programs. Nevertheless, the Agency's defensive reaction to Libya's announcement that it would abandon its nuclear weapons program spoke volumes about the limits of what should be expected of the Agency's capabilities, as well as its unwillingness to acknowledge those limits.[46]

These limitations were evident to the United States and United Kingdom. Throughout the discussions with the Libyans, U.S. and UK intelligence and policy participants emphasized the need for full disclosure and transparency. From March to October 2003, the Libyans initially provided little specific information on their programs, only the promise that more information would be revealed. Once U.S. and UK experts arrived in country, disclosure was generally forthcoming but often incremental. By the end of the second expert visit, there were still unanswered questions and remaining concerns, but all were astonished at how much the Libyans had revealed. The assessment was that sufficient confidence existed to move forward on the policy side, and that even greater confidence would result from the continuing work with the Libyans both on a trilateral basis, as well as from Libya's cooperation with the OPCW and IAEA.

In the President's remarks announcing Libya's decision to abandon WMD, the emphasis on verification remained:

> [Libya] has agreed immediately and unconditionally to allow inspectors from international organizations to enter Libya. These inspectors will render an accounting of all nuclear, chemical and biological weapons programs and will help oversee their elimination. Colonel Ghadafi's commitment, once it is fulfilled, will make our country more safe and the world more peaceful.

Through continuing cooperation after December 2003, even greater confidence has been achieved. Active ongoing monitoring through such measures as the Additional Protocol provides additional ongoing assurances that Libya will not regress on its commitments or, if it does, it will be known.

# *Ensure Secrecy*

Conducting the 10-month dialog with Libya in secrecy was an absolute prerequisite for success. If any hint of these discussions, or of the in-country site visits, had leaked to the media there would almost certainly have been a different outcome. Had the fact of trilateral contacts been revealed publicly, the "angle" played up by the opposition — and likely reflected in the Arab and western press — would have been that Qadaffi was "running scared" to avoid the fate of Saddam. If confronted with this type of news story about abandoning WMD programs, Colonel Qadaffi would have been placed in a defensive position. Opposition to abandonment would have mobilized both internally within Libya and externally, especially within the Arab media. The result would be not only a refusal to admit to the existence of these programs, but also resistance to the removal of the nuclear materials and equipment, as well as elimination of the longer-range missiles for which there were no treaty, political prohibitions, or constraints on Libya.

For this reason, operational knowledge of the contacts with Libya was very tightly restricted from the beginning. At the NSC, only a few individuals were involved. Within the Intelligence Community, there was a strict "need-to-know" rule applied. At State and Defense, knowledge was restricted to the very top level and what was revealed was general in nature. Operational details, including the fact of policy negotiations, were not shared with either department; other departments were even more in the dark. Guidance came directly from the President. Policy (NSC) and Intelligence worked closely at each step to implement the President's direction.

# *Act Fast*

Perhaps a corollary to ensuring secrecy, the U.S. and UK participants understood that speed was essential. A drawn-out process would have increased the prospects for press leaks. Moreover, once the first team was granted access to visit Libya, any delay in moving forward would decrease the pressure on the

Libyan leadership, and could allow time for opposition to mobilize internally and within the region. For this reason, following the second expert site visit in December, U.S. and UK participants pushed for the policy meeting within a few days and, once that meeting achieved the objective of Libyan agreement to publicly acknowledge and abandon its WMD programs, pressed for an early public announcement by the three leaders. The pace in December — moving from the site visit to the statements by the three leaders — was remarkable by any standard of diplomacy.

## *Avoid Bargaining*

A number of Libyan officials have asserted that the decision by Tripoli to abandon its WMD and longer-range missile programs was the outcome of intense bargaining in which the United States and United Kingdom agreed to compensate Libya in a direct and substantial manner. For example, the Secretary of the Libyan General People's Congress, Muhammad al-Zinati, stated publicly in January 2004 that: "Washington would pay a financial or technological compensation in exchange for giving up these components" and that the "United States has promised to defend Libya against any foreign aggression."[47] Such assertions, although often cited by others without direct knowledge of the secret discussions, simply were incorrect.

In the first policy discussion on December 16, the Libyan delegation opened by emphasizing the need to lift U.S. sanctions on Libya once the WMD issue was resolved. The U.S. and UK representatives responded directly that the discussion of sanctions was not the purpose of the meeting and that it would be premature to engage on this subject. U.S. and UK representatives emphasized the need to resolve the WMD issue by recording what must be a strategic decision to eliminate these programs. The vehicle was the draft text of what would be the Libyan statement acknowledging WMD and longer-range missile programs and committing to their elimination.

The U.S. and UK participants took the position from the outset that the very process of bargaining would undercut the prospects for a clear and clean outcome. Bargaining would only slow down the process and likely confuse it. For this reason, such an approach was rejected. Efforts to portray the process as an outcome of classic bargaining, including by Saif al-Islam, simply are inaccurate. (Saif noted in an interview on December 20, 2003, "The truth is that this initiative is a political deal. This is not a secret. It is a political deal; give and take. We give you this much and you give me this much."[48]) More accurate is Colonel Qadaffi's observation that there was no "concrete reward" for giving up the nuclear program.[49] Instead of negotiating X for Y, U.S. and UK representatives insisted that Libya acknowledge and abandon its WMD and longer-range missiles. In doing so, they also made it clear that Libya would remove a major obstacle to improved relations and greater economic and political benefits for the Libyan people.

## *Observations on the Policy/Intelligence Nexus*

The intelligence channel proved to be the best operational vehicle for engagement with Libya as it is inherently compartmented, and can be fast-moving and flexible. It provided U.S. and UK policymakers with an avenue that allowed direct access to Libyan leadership and timely feedback from the Libyans as each step unfolded.

Collaboration between U.S. and UK intelligence was critical to the success of the policy outcome. Working together as a team significantly increased the resources available to the task. Clandestine collection was increased as each service brought its sources to bear; combining experience and skill proved invaluable in moving discussions with the Libyans forward. At the same time, close engagement with the Libyans was crucial. The flexibility of the intelligence channel allowed for continuous contact so that key decision points were pressed forward and the seriousness and urgency of the effort was emphasized over and over.

Throughout the Libyan operation, the operational and analytical synergy obtained by having operators and analysts working side by side also was critical to the successful policy outcome. This integration contributed to the vetting of clandestine sources and helped analysts question and reconsider their assessments when necessary. This was particularly important when the teams entered Libya for the first time in October 2003.

In the Libya case, disruption of supply chain procurement proved essential to success as these operations provided important information and, in turn, leverage which allowed the confident advancement of the policy agenda. This was essential to offset the limitations of technical and national collection efforts. Collection efforts did reveal what the Libyans had in their nuclear program, but there was insufficient information to determine how the Libyans intended to exploit their nuclear materials. In the chemical program, the information collected was good, but the projected quantity of chemical weapons was inaccurate. Prior to the U.S./UK team visits to the various WMD sites, more clandestine sources with access to various facilities would have been more valuable than additional technical or national collection.

Lastly, the intangible concept of operational flow proved once again to be important. The combination of instincts and solid judgment born of operational experience, the acceptance of risk, and the commitment of leadership to success allowed for timely decisions during each of the key engagements with the Libyans. In the intelligence channel, these intangibles should not be underestimated.

# IX. Concluding Thoughts: Responses to the Libyan Model

Given the long-standing investments in their own WMD programs, it is not surprising that North Korea, Iran, and Syria would reject the notion that Libya's decision to abandon WMD and longer-range missiles should serve as an appropriate model for them.

In a January 2005 meeting with the South Korean Foreign Minister, Colonel Qadaffi expressed the view that North Korea and Iran should follow the Libyan model and abandon their nuclear weapons programs. According to press reports, Qadaffi stated that Libya had been trying to convince Pyongyang to give up its weapons programs in exchange for economic and other benefits. According to these reports, the North turned down the offer, emphasizing that it is different from Libya.[50]

Uncharacteristically, Pyongyang was initially slow to respond to the trilateral announcements that Libya had agreed to eliminate all of its WMD programs and longer-range missiles. Perhaps the North was seeking to understand how this decision would affect its missile relationship with Libya. Perhaps it was much more. Reports on December 21, 2003, cited analysts in Seoul who speculated that the Libyan announcement, coming only days after the capture of Saddam and the release of a video showing his pathetic state, had "sent shock waves through the North Korean leadership in its confrontation with the United States over the communist country's nuclear weapons program."[51]

An article published in Tokyo on December 26, 2003, would go even further:

> The awesome gap between the video showing a haggard and miserable Saddam Husayn when he was captured and what he looked like when he was at the peak of power was simply shocking. Barely one week after this, Colonel Qadhafi decided to give up his WMDs in exchange for a security assurance for his

regime.  General Secretary Kim could not possibly have
remained unaffected.   An indication of this is that
the official DPRK [Democratic People's Republic
of Korea] media, including the Korean Central
Broadcasting Station, kept completely silent about
these events.

The author, understanding the dilemma of the North's position,
would also cite a prediction by Pyon Chin-il, chief editor of the *Korea
Report:* "Giving up nuclear arms will mean taking the same course
as Libya, but without nuclear arms, North Korea will be like Iraq,
which was defeated because it did not have nuclear weapons.  It will
not give up so easily."[52]

On January 9, 2004, a North Korean Foreign Ministry
spokesman alluded to the Libyan and Iranian decisions, noting that
Pyongyang would not be influenced by "recent situational
developments" in "some Middle East countries."   By this time North
Korea had recovered all of its usual bravado, announcing that
Washington was "hallucinating" if it believed the North would be
affected by these decisions. On January 11, a signed article in
*Nodong Sinmun* revealed further the North's official reaction:
accepting international inspections, such as was done in Iraq and
perhaps would be done in Libya and Iran, would lead to "sub-
jugation" and would be a "big mistake."[53]

Months later, following high-level calls by the United States
for North Korea to pursue the "Libya model," including by the
President in his visit to Oak Ridge, Pyongyang responded through
an article entitled "Libya-Style Solution." In it, the author declared
that the United States had "ripped out Libya's heart" and that, if the
DPRK were to follow this precedent, the "price it would have to pay
will be the calamity of war and the miserable destiny of a slave."
With rather convoluted logic, the article suggested that Libya paid
an exorbitant price for little return, and that the real U.S. objective
was not to "reward" Libya but to overthrow its regime: "the real intent
of a wolf that has its eyes set on a sheep does not change." In
short, the Libyan model could not apply because the United States
would only be content with the destruction of the North's "system."[54]

The official line that Libya did not benefit from its decision to abandon its nuclear program would become a staple in DPRK public pronouncements. In January 2005, a North Korean publication entitled "Shameless Demand for Following Libyan Example" stated:

> It should be said that Libya has obtained practically nothing as due reward for accepting the United States' demand to renounce nuclear weapons first. Now that Libya has abandoned nuclear weapons, the United States and western countries, which had made a noise as though they would offer some big reward, are barely sparing it a glance, like it were an empty cookie jar... The reality shows that the United States' demand for nuclear weapons renouncement first is a deceptive farce that is only aimed at the disarmament of the other party. That the United States is demanding our Republic also follow "Libya's precedent" despite this is a shameless act.[55]

Iran also would reject the Libyan model but on somewhat different grounds. One initial reaction was to attribute Tripoli's decision to abandon its nuclear weapons program to an obvious attempt by Colonel Qadaffi "simply trying to prolong his stay in power."[56] Another early reaction was to see in the decision "an intricate plot to pressure independent Third World countries in dropping down whatever meager defenses they have against big power aggression and stand stark naked against the onslaught of the armed-to-the teeth U.S., Britain, and the Zionist entity."[57]

In early January 2004, the Iranian position had hardened even further. While portraying Tripoli as a "hostage to American blackmail," Teheran accused Libya of "surrendering" to U.S. "imperialism." Perhaps even more unforgivable, Iran contended that Libya had negotiated a bad deal, giving up something of value without "gaining even minimal concessions." In short, Libya purportedly got a bad deal because it sold too cheaply — in fact, for nothing.[58]

Syria's reaction to the December 2003 announcements was both more direct and more subtle than those of North Korea and Iran. An early reaction came from the highest level. In an interview carried in the London *Daily Telegraph* on January 6, 2004, President

Bashar al-Asad stated that the "surprise" decision by Colonel Qadaffi was a "correct step." He then went on to argue, however, that any agreement to destroy Syria's chemical and biological capabilities would only be feasible if Israel also agreed to abandon its WMD capabilities. In this way, not only did Asad go further than any previous Syrian statement on the possession of WMD, but also appeared to set the conditions for their elimination.[59] Three months later, "Syrian sources" taking part in the March 2003 meetings of Arab Foreign Ministers in Tunis commented publicly that Damascus had rejected a proposal from Tripoli to follow the Libyan example in ending its WMD programs.[60]

The public rejection of the Libyan model by North Korea, Iran, and Syria could easily be anticipated. Each has a set of motivations for, and substantial investments in, its own WMD programs. However, public posturing does not mean that the lessons learned from the Libyan experience do not apply, or cannot be applied, to these and other proliferation challenges. While all three are different from Libya, and from each other, the key is to adapt the lessons learned from Libya to each of these cases in a way that maximizes the prospects for the regimes to make the strategic choice to abandon their WMD programs. This is the lasting value of the Libyan model and its potential contribution to the overall national strategy to combat proliferation of WMD — the preeminent national security threat to the United States, our friends, and allies.

More interesting than the predictable responses of North Korea, Iran, and Syria, is the question of how the lessons of success in Libya have, or have not, been applied by the Bush Administration to other proliferation threats. In May 2007, following a detailed investigation of Tripoli's decision to give up its WMD and longer-range missile programs, Judith Miller wrote in *The National Interest*:

> The Bush Administration can point to only one un-deniable non-proliferation "success" so far in its tenure: Libya's decision to renounce WMD in December 2003. But the administration that so adroitly pushed Libya to abandon unconventional weapons has been unable, or in some cases unwilling, to apply the key lessons of that success to its other nuclear challenges.[61]

While some of the lessons learned from Libya may be tactical in nature and others unique to the circumstances that existed in the spring and fall of 2003, a number of the identified lessons clearly apply to today's proliferation challenges.   In particular, five appear essential to success:

- Demonstration of Seriousness
- Insistence on a Strategic Decision
- Employment of all Tools (Diplomacy, Economic/ Financial, Interdiction, Military)
- Creation of a Win-Win Outcome
- Assurance of Complete and Continuing Access for Verification

Knowing whether and, if so, why and how these lessons have influenced U.S. policy toward North Korea, Iran, and Syria could add significantly to an understanding of U.S. non- and counter-proliferation policies. This is a topic that merits additional research and analysis.

# End Notes

1.  See, for example, Malfrid Braut-Hegghammer, "Libya's Nuclear Turnaround: Perspectives from Tripoli," Middle East Journal, Volume 20, No. 1, Winter 2008; Sharon Squassoni and Andrew Feickert, "Disarming Libya: Weapons of Mass Destruction," Congressional Research Service, April 22, 2004, and, John Hart and Shannon Kile, "Libya's Renunciation of Nuclear, Biological and Chemical Weapons and Ballistic Missiles," Armaments, Disarmament and International Security, SIPRI Yearbook, 2005. A more comprehensive treatment of the motivations surrounding both Libya's pursuit of nuclear weapons as well as its decision to abandon them can be found in, Wyn Q. Bowen, "Libya and Nuclear Proliferation," Adelphi Paper 380, The International Institute for Strategic Studies, May 2006.

2.  The White House, Remarks by President George W. Bush at the National Defense University, May 1, 2001, available from http://www. whitehouse.gov/news/releases/2001/05/20010501-10.html

3.  The White House, The National Security Strategy of the United States of America, September 17, 2002, available from http://www.whitehouse. gov/nsc/nss/2002/nss.pdf.

4.  The White House, National Strategy to Combat Weapons of Mass Destruction, December 11, 2002, available from www.whitehouse.gov/ news/releases/2002/12/WMDStrategy.pdf.

5.  Paris, l'Agence France Presse (AFP), May 17, 2003. See also Novinite, January 27, 2003.

6.  The White House, Remarks by President George W. Bush to the People of Poland, Krakow, Poland, May 31, 2003, available from http:// www.whitehouse.gov/news/releases/2003/05/20030531-3.html.

7.  Panafrican News Agency (PANA), January 2, 2003.

8.  Tripoli, Great Jamahiriyah TV, in Arabic, 0030 GMT 20 March 2003, Foreign Broadcast Information Service (FBIS) text.

9.  "O Iraq of History, May God Protect You," London, al-Arab al-Alamiyah, in Arabic, April 10, 2003.

10.  Tripoli, Jamahiriya News Agency (JANA), in Arabic, 0019 GMT 13 October 2002.

11.  "Libyan Paper Urges Activation of Union Between Libya, Egypt,

Sudan," Cairo, Middle East News Agency (MENA), in English, 1352 GMT, 9 May 2003, FBIS text.

12.   Lally Weymouth. "The Former Face of Evil: Muammar Kaddafi on the Pan Am 103 Bombing, the Fate of Saddam Hussein and Weapons of Mass Destruction," Newsweek, January 20, 2003, p. 36.

13.   Agence France Presse, January 9, 2003.

14.   Charles Lambroschini, "Interview: Libyan Leader Muammar al-Qaddafi,'" Paris, Le Figaro, March 11, 2003, available from http://www.worldpress.org.

15.   U.S. Department of State, Statement by Secretary Colin Powell, August 15, 2003, available from http://www.america.gov/st/washfile-english/2003/August/20030817133140uhp5.929202E-02.html.

16.   White House Press Release, Office of the Press Secretary, August 15, 2003, available from http://www.america.gov/st/washfile-english/2003/August/20030815185733namfuaks0.9970209.html.

17.   House International Relations Committee, Hearing on Disarming Weapons of Mass Destruction in Libya, Federal Document Clearing House transcript, September 22, 2004, available from http://commdocs.house.gov/committees/intlrel/hfa95978.000/hfa95978_Of.html.

18.   Boris Johnson and Nicholas Farrell, "Let Us Export Democracy by Force," interview with Prime Minister Berlusconi, Il Corriere di Firenze, September 4, 2003, FBIS text; and Robin Gedye, "UN Should Fight for Rights, Says Berlusconi," London Daily Telegraph, September 9, 2003, p. 16.

19.   CIA: "The Worldwide Threat 2004: Challenges in a Changing Global Context," Testimony of Director of Central Intelligence, George J. Tenet, before the Senate Armed Services Committee, 9 March 2004, as prepared, available from http://www.cia.gov/news-information/speeches-testimony/2004/tenet testimony 03092004.html.

20.   CIA: "Unclassified Report to Congress on the Acquisition of Technology Relating to Weapons of Mass Destruction and Advanced Conventional Munitions, 1 January Through 30 June 2001," available from http://www.cia.gov/library/reports/archived-reports-1/jan jun2001.html.

21.   CIA: "Unclassified Report to Congress on the Acquisition of Technology Relating to Weapons of Mass Destruction and Advanced Conventional Munitions, 1 January Through 30 June 2002," available from http://www.cia.gov/library/reports/archived-reports-1/jan jun2002.html.

22.   CIA: "Unclassified Report to Congress on the Acquisition of Technology Relating to Weapons of Mass Destruction and Advanced Conventional Munitions, 1 January Through 30 June 2003," available from http://www.cia.gov/library/reports/archived-reports-1/jan jun2003. html.

23.   CIA: "DCI's Worldwide Threat Briefing," February 11, 2003 ("The Worldwide Threat: Evolving Dangers in a Complex World"), available from http://www.cia.gov/news-information/speeches-testimony/2003/ dci_speech_02112003.html.

24.   "Diplomats: Libya to Sign Protocol Allowing Surprise Nuclear Inspections by UN," Paris, AFP, in English, December 21, 2003.

25.   CIA: "Unclassified Report to Congress on the Acquisition of Technology Relating to Weapons of Mass Destruction and Advanced Conventional Munitions 1 July through 31 December 2003," available from http://www.cia.gov/library/reports/archived-reports-1/july dec2003. html.

26.   Press reports suggest that British Intelligence responded "bluntly" to this initial offer, noting that Libya's WMD would have to go or Libya would be attacked. Gordon Thomas, "What's Up with Gadaffi?" 28 December 2003, www.solomonstemple.com.

27.   Al-Jazirah, 20 December 2003, FBIS text.

28.   Peter Beaumont, Kamal Ahmed, and Martin Bright, "Deal with Gadaffi: The Meeting that Brought Libya in from the Cold," Observer, December 21, 2003, p. 6.

29.   The White House, Office of the Press Secretary, December 19, 2003, available from http://www.fas.org/nuke/guide/libya/wh121903fs. html.

30.   Donald Mahley, "Dismantling Libyan Lessons: Lessons Learned," paper presented at Wilton House Conference, October 8-10, 2004, available from http://cbaci.org.

31.   "Libya, Iraq and Iran: Updates and Analyses," The Acronym Institute, Issue No. 77, May/June 2004.

32.   U.S. Department of State, "Libya Ending Military Trade with States of Serious Weapons of Mass Destruction Proliferation Concern," Excerpt from Daily Press Briefing, May 13, 2004, available from http://www.state. gov/p/nea/rls/32491.html.

33.   Excerpt from Daily Press Briefing, Department of State, May 13, 2004.

34.   The White House, Remarks by President George W. Bush on the

War on Terror, Oak Ridge National Laboratory, Oak Ridge, Tennessee, July 12, 2004, available from http://www.whitehouse.gov/news/releases/2004/07/20040712-5.html.

35.   Rome, Radiotelevisione Italiana (RAI) Television Network 2300 17 December 2004, FBIS text.

36.   Mahley, *op cit.*

37.   Al-Jazirah, 26 December 2003, FBIS text.

38.   Patrice Claude, "According to His Son, Colonel al-Qadhdhafi Did Not Abandon Nuclear Because of War on Saddam," Paris, Le Monde, 11 February 2004, FBIS text.

39.   London Times, January 4, 2004.

40.   Mahley, *op cit.*

41.   "Diplomacy, Not War on Iraq, Forced Libya to Give Up Nuclear Quest: Blix," Paris, AFP, January 29, 2004.

42.   Tripoli, Great Jamahiriyah TV, 7 January 2004, FBIS text.

43.   Aminah Nasr,   "Libyan Decision Viewed as Real Success for Al-Qaddafi; Reward Expected," Cairo, Al-Ahram, 3 January 2004, FBIS text.

44.   FBIS text, 30 December 2004.

45.   See, interview with Ibrahim Sahd, Deputy Head of the People's Front for the Salvation of Libya, in Cairo, 4 January 2004, FBIS text.

46.   Nasr, *op cit.*

47.   "Al-Majallah Interview: Libyan Parliament Secretary on Rapprochement with U.S." London, Al-Majallah, 18 January 2004, FBIS text.

48.   Al-Jazirah, 20 December 2003, FBIS text.

49.   FBIS text, 12 December 2003.

50.   "Husayn, Qadhafi Capitulating to U.S.: What Will General Secretary Kim Chong-il Do Next?" Tokyo Shimbun, internet version in Japanese, 26 December 2003, FBIS text.

51.   "ROK Foreign Minister: Libya's 'Case' Could Be 'Good Reference' for DPRK," Seoul Yonhap, in English, 0256 GMT 21 December 2003, FBIS text.

52.   "Husayn, Qadhafi Capitulating to US: What Will General Secretary Kim Chong-il Do Next?" *op cit.*

53.   "DPRK Reacts to Middle East 'Developments,' Warns of 'Pacifistic Mood'," Foreign Media Notes (FMN) in English, 16 January 2004, FBIS text.

54.   "Libya Style Solution Not Fit for Circumstances of Korea," Pyongyang T'ongil Sinbo, internet version in Korean, 14 August 2002.

55. Pyongyang, T'ongil Sinbo, 15 January 2005, FBIS text.

56. "Iranian Paper Says Libyan Move Shows Al-Qadhafi's Desire to Stay in Power," Teheran Iran News, 21 December, 2003, FBIS text.

57. S. Nawabzadeh. "Iran: Editorial Hits US, UK 'Bragging' Over Libyan Decision to Dismantle WMD," Teheran Keyhan International, 21 December 2003, FBIS text.

58. "Program Summary: Tehran Vision of Iran Network 1," 1030 GMT, 6 January 2004, FBIS text.

59. Benedict Brogan, "We Won't Scrap WMD Stockpile Unless Israel Does, Says Assad," The Daily Telegraph, 5 January 2004, p. 1.

60. "Syrian Sources: Syria Rejected Libyan Plan to Follow Its Example, Remove WMD," London, Al-Sharq al-Awast, 27 March 2004.

61. Judith Miller, "From the Shores of Tripoli," The National Interest, Volume 89, May/June 2007, p. 26.

## ANNEX A

## Remarks by President George W. Bush to Students and Faculty at National Defense University, May 1, 2001

Fort Lesley J. McNair
Washington, D.C.
1 May 2001

THE PRESIDENT: Thank you very much, Mr. Secretary. I appreciate you being here. I also want to thank Secretary Powell for being here as well. My National Security Advisor, Condi Rice is here, as well as the Vice Chairman of the Joint Chiefs, General Myers. I appreciate Admiral Clark and General Ryan here, for being here as well. But most of all, I want to thank you, Admiral Gaffney, and the students of NDU for having me here today.

For almost 100 years, this campus has served as one of our country's premier centers for learning and thinking about America's national security. Some of America's finest soldiers have studied here: Dwight Eisenhower and Colin Powell. Some of America's finest statesmen have taught here; George Kennan. Today, you're carrying on this proud tradition forward, continuing to train tomorrow's generals, admirals and other national security thinkers, and continuing to provide the intellectual capital for our nation's strategic vision.

This afternoon, I want us to think back some 30 years to a far different time in a far different world. The United States and the Soviet Union were locked in a hostile rivalry. The Soviet Union was our unquestioned enemy; a highly-armed threat to freedom and democracy. Far more than that wall in Berlin divided us.

Our highest ideal was — and remains — individual liberty. Theirs was the construction of a vast communist empire. Their totalitarian regime held much of Europe captive behind an Iron Curtain.

We didn't trust them, and for good reason. Our deep differences were expressed in a dangerous military confrontation that resulted in thousands of nuclear weapons pointed at each other on hair-trigger alert. Security of both the United States and the Soviet Union was based on a grim premise: that neither side would fire nuclear weapons at each other, because doing so would mean the end of both nations.

We even went so far as to codify this relationship in a 1972 ABM Treaty, based on the doctrine that our very survival would best be insured by leaving both sides completely open and vulnerable to nuclear attack. The threat was real and vivid. The Strategic Air Command had an airborne command post called the Looking Glass, aloft 24 hours a day, ready in case the President ordered our strategic forces to move toward their targets and release their nuclear ordnance.

The Soviet Union had almost 1.5 million troops deep in the heart of Europe, in Poland and Czechoslovakia, Hungary and East Germany. We used our nuclear weapons not just to prevent the Soviet Union from using their nuclear weapons, but also to contain their conventional military forces, to prevent them from extending the Iron Curtain into parts of Europe and Asia that were still free.

In that world, few other nations had nuclear weapons and most of those who did were responsible allies, such as Britain and France. We worried about the proliferation of nuclear weapons to other countries, but it was mostly a distant threat, not yet a reality.

Today, the sun comes up on a vastly different world. The Wall is gone, and so is the Soviet Union. Today's Russia is not yesterday's Soviet Union. Its government is no longer Communist. Its president is elected. Today's Russia is not our enemy, but a country in transition with an opportunity to emerge as a great nation, democratic, at peace with itself and its neighbors. The Iron Curtain no longer exists. Poland, Hungary and the Czech Republic are free nations, and they are now our allies in NATO, together with a reunited Germany.

Yet, this is still a dangerous world, a less certain, a less predictable one. More nations have nuclear weapons and still more have nuclear aspirations. Many have chemical and biological weapons. Some already have developed the ballistic missile technology that would allow them to deliver weapons of mass destruction at long distances and at incredible speeds. And a number of these countries are spreading these technologies around the world.

Most troubling of all, the list of these countries includes some of the world's least responsible states. Unlike the Cold War, today's most urgent threat stems not from thousands of ballistic missiles in the Soviet hands, but from a small number of missiles in the hands of these states, states for whom terror and blackmail are a way of life. They seek weapons of mass destruction to intimidate their neighbors, and to keep the United States and other responsible nations from helping allies and friends in strategic parts of the world.

When Saddam Hussein invaded Kuwait in 1990, the world joined forces to turn him back. But the international community would have faced a very different situation had Hussein been able to blackmail with nuclear weapons. Like Saddam Hussein, some of today's tyrants are gripped by an implacable hatred of the United States of America. They hate our friends, they hate our values, they hate democracy and freedom and individual liberty. Many care little for the lives of their own people. In such a world, Cold War deterrence is no longer enough.

To maintain peace, to protect our own citizens and our own allies and friends, we must seek security based on more than the grim premise that we can destroy those who seek to destroy us. This is an important opportunity for the world to re-think the unthinkable, and to find new ways to keep the peace.

Today's world requires a new policy, a broad strategy of active nonproliferation, counterproliferation and defenses. We must work together with other like-minded nations to deny weapons of terror from those seeking to acquire them. We must work with allies and friends who wish to join with us to defend against the harm they can inflict. And together we must deter anyone who would contemplate their use.

We need new concepts of deterrence that rely on both offensive and defensive forces. Deterrence can no longer be based solely on the threat of nuclear retaliation. Defenses can strengthen deterrence by reducing the incentive for proliferation.

We need a new framework that allows us to build missile defenses to counter the different threats of today's world. To do so, we must move beyond the constraints of the 30-year-old ABM Treaty. This treaty does not recognize the present, or point us to the future.

It enshrines the past. No treaty that prevents us from addressing today's threats, that prohibits us from pursuing promising technology to defend ourselves, our friends and our allies is in our interests or in the interests of world peace.

This new framework must encourage still further cuts in nuclear weapons. Nuclear weapons still have a vital role to play in our security and that of our allies. We can, and will, change the size, the composition, the character of our nuclear forces in a way that reflects the reality that the Cold War is over.

I am committed to achieving a credible deterrent with the lowest-possible number of nuclear weapons consistent with our national security needs, including our obligations to our allies. My goal is to move quickly to reduce nuclear forces. The United States will lead by example to achieve our interests and the interests for peace in the world.

Several months ago, I asked Secretary of Defense Rumsfeld to examine all available technologies and basing modes for effective missile defenses that could protect the United States, our deployed forces, our friends and our allies. The Secretary has explored a number of complementary and innovative approaches.

The Secretary has identified near-term options that could allow us to deploy an initial capability against limited threats. In some cases, we can draw on already established technologies that might involve land-based and sea-based capabilities to intercept missiles in mid-course or after they re-enter the atmosphere. We also recognize the substantial advantages of intercepting missiles early in their flight, especially in the boost phase.

The preliminary work has produced some promising options for advanced sensors and interceptors that may provide this capability. If based at sea or on aircraft, such approaches could provide limited, but effective, defenses.

We have more work to do to determine the final form the defenses might take. We will explore all these options further. We recognize the technological difficulties we face and we look forward to the challenge. Our nation will assign the best people to this critical task.

We will evaluate what works and what does not. We know that some approaches will not work. We also know that we will be able to build on our successes. When ready, and working with Congress, we will deploy missile defenses to strengthen global security and stability.

I've made it clear from the very beginning that I would consult closely on the important subject with our friends and allies who are also threatened by missiles and weapons of mass destruction.

Today, I'm announcing the dispatch of high-level representatives to Allied capitals in Europe, Asia, Australia and Canada to discuss our common responsibility to create a new framework for security and stability that reflects the world of today. They will begin leaving next week.

The delegations will be headed by three men on this stage: Rich Armitage, Paul Wolfowitz, and Steve Hadley; Deputies of the State Department, the Defense Department and the National Security staff. Their trips will be part of an ongoing process of consultation, involving many people and many levels of government, including my Cabinet Secretaries.

These will be real consultations. We are not presenting our friends and allies with unilateral decisions already made. We look forward to hearing their views, the views of our friends, and to take them into account.

We will seek their input on all the issues surrounding the new strategic environment. We'll also need to reach out to other interested states, including China and Russia. Russia and the United States should work together to develop a new foundation for world peace and security in the 21st century. We should leave behind the constraints of an ABM Treaty that perpetuates a relationship based on distrust and mutual vulnerability. This Treaty ignores the fundamental breakthroughs in technology during the last 30 years. It prohibits us from exploring all options for defending against the threats that face us, our allies and other countries.

That's why we should work together to replace this Treaty with a new framework that reflects a clear and clean break from the past, and especially from the adversarial legacy of the Cold War. This new cooperative relationship should look to the future, not to the past. It should be reassuring, rather than threatening. It should be premised on openness, mutual confidence and real opportunities for cooperation, including the area of missile defense. It should allow us to share information so that each nation can improve its early warning capability, and its capability to defend its people and territory. And perhaps one day, we can even cooperate in a joint defense.

I want to complete the work of changing our relationship from one based on a nuclear balance of terror, to one based on common responsibilities and common interests. We may have areas of difference with Russia, but we are not and must not be strategic adversaries. Russia and America both face new threats to security. Together, we can address today's threats and pursue today's opportunities. We can explore technologies that have the potential to make us all safer.

This is a time for vision; a time for a new way of thinking; a time for bold leadership. The Looking Glass no longer stands its 24-hour-day vigil. We must all look at the world in a new, realistic way, to preserve peace for generations to come.

God bless.

# *ANNEX B*

# National Strategy to Combat Weapons of Mass Destruction, December 11, 2002

*The gravest danger our Nation faces lies at the crossroads of radicalism and technology. Our enemies have openly declared that they are seeking weapons of mass destruction, and evidence indicates that they are doing so with determination. The United States will not allow these efforts to succeed. ...History will judge harshly those who saw this coming danger but failed to act. In the new world we have entered, the only path to peace and security is the path of action.*

President Bush
The National Security Strategy of the United States of America
September 17, 2002

## Introduction

Weapons of mass destruction (WMD) — nuclear, biological, and chemical — in the possession of hostile states and terrorists represent one of the greatest security challenges facing the United States. We must pursue a comprehensive strategy to counter this threat in all of its dimensions.

An effective strategy for countering WMD, including their use and further proliferation, is an integral component of the National Security Strategy of the United States of America. As with the war on terrorism, our strategy for homeland security, and our new concept of deterrence, the U.S. approach to combat WMD represents a fundamental change from the past. To succeed, we must take full advantage of today's opportunities, including the application of new technologies, increased emphasis on intelligence collection and analysis, the strengthening of alliance relationships, and the establishment of new partnerships with former adversaries.

Weapons of mass destruction could enable adversaries to inflict massive harm on the United States, our military forces at home and abroad, and our friends and allies. Some states, including several that have supported and continue to support terrorism, already possess WMD and are seeking even greater capabilities, as tools of coercion and intimidation. For them, these are not weapons of last resort, but militarily useful weapons of choice intended to overcome our nation's advantages in conventional forces and to deter us from responding to aggression against our friends and allies in regions of vital interest. In addition, terrorist groups are seeking to acquire WMD with the stated purpose of killing large numbers of our people and those of friends and allies — without compunction and without warning.

We will not permit the world's most dangerous regimes and terrorists to threaten us with the world's most destructive weapons. We must accord the highest priority to the protection of the United States, our forces, and our friends and allies from the existing and growing WMD threat.

## Pillars of our National Strategy

Our National Strategy to Combat Weapons of Mass Destruction has three principal pillars:

### 1. Counterproliferation to Combat WMD Use

The possession and increased likelihood of use of WMD by hostile states and terrorists are realities of the contemporary security environment. It is therefore critical that the U. S. military and appropriate civilian agencies be prepared to deter and defend against the full range of possible WMD employment scenarios. We will ensure that all needed capabilities to combat WMD are fully integrated into the emerging defense transformation plan and into our homeland security posture. Counterproliferation will also be fully integrated into the basic doctrine, training, and equipping of all forces, in order to ensure that they can sustain operations to decisively defeat WMD-armed adversaries.

## 2. Strengthened Nonproliferation to Combat WMD Proliferation

The United States, our friends and allies, and the broader international community must undertake every effort to prevent states and terrorists from acquiring WMD and missiles. We must enhance traditional measures — diplomacy, arms control, multilateral agreements, threat reduction assistance, and export controls — that seek to dissuade or impede proliferant states and terrorist networks, as well as to slow and make more costly their access to sensitive technologies, material, and expertise. We must ensure compliance with relevant international agreements, including the Nuclear Nonproliferation Treaty (NPT), the Chemical Weapons Convention (CWC), and the Biological Weapons Convention (BWC). The United States will continue to work with other states to improve their capability to prevent un-authorized transfers of WMD and missile technology, expertise, and material. We will identify and pursue new methods of prevention, such as national criminalization of proliferation activities and expanded safety and security measures.

## 3. Consequence Management to Respond to WMD Use

Finally, the United States must be prepared to respond to the use of WMD against our citizens, our military forces, and those of friends and allies. We will develop and maintain the capability to reduce to the extent possible the potentially horrific consequences of WMD attacks at home and abroad.

The three pillars of the U.S. national strategy to combat WMD are seamless elements of a comprehensive approach. Serving to integrate the pillars are four cross-cutting enabling functions that need to be pursued on a priority basis: intelligence collection and analysis on WMD, delivery systems, and related technologies; research and development to improve our ability to respond to evolving threats; bilateral and multilateral cooperation; and targeted strategies against hostile states and terrorists.

# 1. Counterproliferation

We know from experience that we cannot always be successful in preventing and containing the proliferation of WMD to hostile states and terrorists. Therefore, U.S. military and appropriate civilian agencies must possess the full range of operational capabilities to counter the threat and use of WMD by states and terrorists against the United States, our military forces, and friends and allies.

## *Interdiction*

Effective interdiction is a critical part of the U.S. strategy to combat WMD and their delivery means. We must enhance the capabilities of our military, intelligence, technical, and law enforcement communities to prevent the movement of WMD materials, technology, and expertise to hostile states and terrorist organizations.

## *Deterrence*

Today's threats are far more diverse and less predictable than those of the past. States hostile to the United States and to our friends and allies have demonstrated their willingness to take high risks to achieve their goals, and are aggressively pursuing WMD and their means of delivery as critical tools in this effort. As a consequence, we require new methods of deterrence. A strong declaratory policy and effective military forces are essential elements of our contemporary deterrent posture, along with the full range of political tools to persuade potential adversaries not to seek or use WMD. The United States will continue to make clear that it reserves the right to respond with overwhelming force — including through resort to all of our options — to the use of WMD against the United States, our forces abroad, and friends and allies.

In addition to our conventional and nuclear response and defense capabilities, our overall deterrent posture against WMD threats is reinforced by effective intelligence, surveillance, interdiction, and domestic law enforcement capabilities. Such combined capabilities enhance deterrence both by devaluing an adversary's WMD and missiles, and by posing the prospect of an overwhelming response to any use of such weapons.

## *Defense and Mitigation*

Because deterrence may not succeed, and because of the potentially devastating consequences of WMD use against our forces and civilian population, U.S. military forces and appropriate civilian agencies must have the capability to defend against WMD-armed adversaries, including in appropriate cases through preemptive measures. This requires capabilities to detect and destroy an adversary's WMD assets before these weapons are used. In addition, robust active and passive defenses and mitigation measures must be in place to enable U.S. military forces and appropriate civilian agencies to accomplish their missions, and to assist friends and allies when WMD are used.

Active defenses disrupt, disable, or destroy WMD en route to their targets. Active defenses include vigorous air defense and effective missile defenses against today's threats. Passive defenses must be tailored to the unique characteristics of the various forms of WMD. The United States must also have the ability rapidly and effectively to mitigate the effects of a WMD attack against our deployed forces.

Our approach to defend against biological threats has long been based on our approach to chemical threats, despite the fundamental differences between these weapons. The United States is developing a new approach to provide us and our friends and allies with an effective defense against biological weapons.

Finally, U.S. military forces and domestic law enforcement agencies as appropriate must stand ready to respond against the source of any WMD attack. The primary objective of a response is to disrupt an imminent attack or an attack in progress, and eliminate the threat of future attacks. As with deterrence and prevention, an effective response requires rapid attribution and robust strike capability. We must accelerate efforts to field new capabilities to defeat WMD-related assets. The United States needs to be prepared to conduct post-conflict operations to destroy or dismantle any residual WMD capabilities of the hostile state or terrorist network. An effective U.S. response not only will eliminate the source of a WMD attack but will also have a powerful deterrent effect upon other adversaries that possess or seek WMD or missiles.

# 2. Nonproliferation

## *Active Nonproliferation Diplomacy*

The United States will actively employ diplomatic approaches in bilateral and multilateral settings in pursuit of our nonproliferation goals. We must dissuade supplier states from cooperating with proliferant states and induce proliferant states to end their WMD and missile programs. We will hold countries responsible for complying with their commitments. In addition, we will continue to build coalitions to support our efforts, as well as to seek their increased support for nonproliferation and threat reduction cooperation programs. However, should our wide-ranging nonproliferation efforts fail, we must have available the full range of operational capabilities necessary to defend against the possible employment of WMD.

## *Multilateral Regimes*

Existing nonproliferation and arms control regimes play an important role in our overall strategy. The United States will support those regimes that are currently in force, and work to improve the effectiveness of, and compliance with, those regimes. Consistent with other policy priorities, we will also promote new agreements and arrangements that serve our nonproliferation goals. Overall, we seek to cultivate an international environment that is more conducive to nonproliferation. Our efforts will include:

- Nuclear
    - o Strengthening of the Nuclear Nonproliferation Treaty and International Atomic Energy Agency (IAEA), including through ratification of an IAEA Additional Protocol by all NPT states parties, assurances that all states put in place full-scope IAEA safeguards agreements, and appropriate increases in funding for the Agency;
    - o Negotiating a Fissile Material Cut-Off Treaty that advances U.S. security interests; and

- o Strengthening the Nuclear Suppliers Group and Zangger Committee.

- Chemical and Biological

  - o Effective functioning of the Organization for the Prohibition of Chemical Weapons;
  - o Identification and promotion of constructive and realistic measures to strengthen the BWC and thereby to help meet the biological weapons threat; and
  - o Strengthening of the Australia Group.

- Missile

  - o Strengthening the Missile Technology Control Regime (MTCR), including through support for universal adherence to the International Code of Conduct Against Ballistic Missile Proliferation.

## *Nonproliferation and Threat Reduction Cooperation*

The United States pursues a wide range of programs, including the Nunn-Lugar program, designed to address the proliferation threat stemming from the large quantities of Soviet-legacy WMD and missile-related expertise and materials. Maintaining an extensive and efficient set of nonproliferation and threat reduction assistance programs with Russia and other former Soviet states is a high priority. We will also continue to encourage friends and allies to increase their contributions to these programs, particularly through the G-8 Global Partnership Against the Spread of Weapons and Materials of Mass Destruction. In addition, we will work with other states to improve the security of their WMD-related materials.

## *Controls on Nuclear Materials*

In addition to programs with former Soviet states to reduce fissile material and improve the security of that which remains, the United States will continue to discourage the worldwide accumulation of separated plutonium and to minimize the use of highly-enriched uranium. As outlined in the National Energy Policy, the United

States will work in collaboration with international partners to develop recycle and fuel treatment technologies that are cleaner, more efficient, less waste-intensive, and more proliferation-resistant.

## U.S. Export Controls

We must ensure that the implementation of U.S. export controls furthers our nonproliferation and other national security goals, while recognizing the realities that American businesses face in the increasingly globalized marketplace.

We will work to update and strengthen export controls using existing authorities. We also seek new legislation to improve the ability of our export control system to give full weight to both nonproliferation objectives and commercial interests. Our overall goal is to focus our resources on truly sensitive exports to hostile states or those that engage in onward proliferation, while removing un-necessary barriers in the global marketplace.

## Nonproliferation Sanctions

Sanctions can be a valuable component of our overall strategy against WMD proliferation. At times, however, sanctions have proven inflexible and ineffective. We will develop a comprehensive sanctions policy to better integrate sanctions into our overall strategy and work with Congress to consolidate and modify existing sanctions legislation.

## 3. WMD Consequence Management

Defending the American homeland is the most basic responsibility of our government. As part of our defense, the United States must be fully prepared to respond to the consequences of WMD use on our soil, whether by hostile states or by terrorists. We must also be prepared to respond to the effects of WMD use against our forces deployed abroad, and to assist friends and allies.

The National Strategy for Homeland Security discusses U.S. Government programs to deal with the consequences of the use of a chemical, biological, radiological, or nuclear weapon in the United States. A number of these programs offer training, planning, and assistance to state and local governments. To maximize their effectiveness, these efforts need to be integrated and comprehensive. Our first responders must have the full range of protective, medical, and remediation tools to identify, assess, and respond rapidly to a WMD event on our territory.

The White House Office of Homeland Security will coordinate all federal efforts to prepare for and mitigate the consequences of terrorist attacks within the United States, including those involving WMD. The Office of Homeland Security will also work closely with state and local governments to ensure their planning, training, and equipment requirements are addressed. These issues, including the roles of the Department of Homeland Security, are addressed in detail in the National Strategy for Homeland Security.

The National Security Council's Office of Combating Terrorism coordinates and helps improve U.S. efforts to respond to and manage the recovery from terrorist attacks outside the United States. In cooperation with the Office of Combating Terrorism, the Department of State coordinates interagency efforts to work with our friends and allies to develop their own emergency preparedness and consequence management capabilities.

## Integrating the Pillars

Several critical enabling functions serve to integrate the three pillars — counterproliferation, nonproliferation, and consequence management — of the U.S. National Strategy to Combat WMD.

### *Improved Intelligence Collection and Analysis*

A more accurate and complete understanding of the full range of WMD threats is, and will remain, among the highest U. S. intelligence priorities, to enable us to prevent proliferation, and to deter or defend against those who would use those capabilities against us. Improving our ability to obtain timely and accurate knowledge of adversaries' offensive and defensive capabilities, plans, and intentions is key to developing effective counter- and nonproliferation policies and capabilities. Particular emphasis must be accorded to improving: intelligence regarding WMD-related facilities and activities;

interaction among U.S. intelligence, law enforcement, and military agencies; and intelligence cooperation with friends and allies.

## Research and Development

The United States has a critical need for cutting-edge technology that can quickly and effectively detect, analyze, facilitate interdiction of, defend against, defeat, and mitigate the consequences of WMD. Numerous U.S. Government departments and agencies are currently engaged in the essential research and development to support our overall strategy against WMD proliferation.

The new Counterproliferation Technology Coordination Committee, consisting of senior representatives from all concerned agencies, will act to improve interagency coordination of U.S. Government counterproliferation research and development efforts. The Committee will assist in identifying priorities, gaps, and overlaps in existing programs and in examining options for future investment strategies.

## Strengthened International Cooperation

WMD represent a threat not just to the United States, but also to our friends and allies and the broader international community. For this reason, it is vital that we work closely with like-minded countries on all elements of our comprehensive proliferation strategy.

## Targeted Strategies Against Proliferants

All elements of the overall U. S. strategy to combat WMD must be brought to bear in targeted strategies against supplier and recipient states of WMD proliferation concern, as well as against terrorist groups which seek to acquire WMD.

A few states are dedicated proliferators, whose leaders are determined to develop, maintain, and improve their WMD and delivery capabilities, which directly threaten the United States, U.S. forces overseas, and/or our friends and allies. Because each of these regimes is different, we will pursue country-specific strategies that best enable us and our friends and allies to prevent, deter, and defend against WMD and missile threats from each of them. These strategies must also take into account the growing cooperation among proliferant states — so-called secondary proliferation — which challenges us to think in new ways about specific country strategies.

One of the most difficult challenges we face is to prevent, deter, and defend against the acquisition and use of WMD by terrorist groups. The current and potential future linkages between terrorist groups and state sponsors of terrorism are particularly dangerous and require priority attention. The full range of counterproliferation, nonproliferation, and consequence management measures must be brought to bear against the WMD terrorist threat, just as they are against states of greatest proliferation concern.

## End Note

Our National Strategy to Combat WMD requires much of all of us — the Executive Branch, the Congress, state and local governments, the American people, and our friends and allies. The requirements to prevent, deter, defend against, and respond to today's WMD threats are complex and challenging. But they are not daunting. We can and will succeed in the tasks laid out in this strategy; we have no other choice.

# ANNEX C

# U.S./UK/Libyan Declarations, December 19, 2003

## Statement by the Libyan Foreign Minister:

Because of the international climate that prevailed during the Cold War, as well as the tension within the Middle East region, Libya called on states in the region to make the Middle East and Africa a WMD free zone. In view of the fact that this call did not receive a serious response, Libya worked to develop its capabilities.

Libyan experts have held discussions with experts from the US and UK about Libya's activities in this field. The Libyan experts showed their counterparts from the US and UK the materials, equipments and programmes which led to the productions of internationally proscribed weapons. These included centrifuge machines and chemical munitions.

And on the basis of these discussions which Libya held with the US and UK both of which are permanent members of the UN Security Council responsible for guaranteeing international peace and security. Libya, of its own free will, has decided to eliminate these materials, equipments and programmes so that Libya may be completely free of internationally proscribed weapons.

And Libya has decided to restrict itself to missiles with a range in accordance with the standards agreed in the MTCR. Libya will take these steps with all verifiable transparency, including immediate international inspections.

In addition to this, we wish to confirm that Libya will be bound by the NPT, the Safeguards Agreement of the IAEA and Additional Protocol of the IAEA and the Biological Weapons Convention. And it will accept any other obligations including the Additional Protocol of the IAEA Safeguards Agreement and the Chemical Weapons Convention.

Libya's belief is that an arms race does not serve its security nor the security of the region, but conflicts with Libya's great concern for the world blessed with security and peace. Libya's desire of this initiative is that all states will follow Libya's model, beginning with the Middle East region without double standards.

Libya will inform the UN Security Council of this.

## Statement Released in the Name of Colonel Qadaffi:

The statement made by the Secretary for the General People's Committee for Foreign Liaison and International Cooperation is considered a wise decision and a brave step that merits the support of the Libyan people, showing that Libya has taken the initiative and has instigated among the countries of the world especially the Middle East, Africa, and the Third World, the abandonment of WMD programmes and that the Jamahiriyah should play an international role in building a new world void of WMD and void of all types of terrorism, with the aim of international peacekeeping and the advancement of humanity in the fields of development, people's democracy and facing environmental challenges, so that the colour green will be all over the world.

## Statement by Prime Minister Blair:

This evening Colonel Qadhafi has confirmed that Libya has in the past sought to develop WMD capabilities, as well as longer-range missiles. Libya came to us in March following successful negotiations on Lockerbie to see if it could resolve its WMD issue in a similarly co-operative manner. Nine months of work followed with experts from the US and UK, during which the Libyans discussed their programmes with us. As a result, Libya has now declared its intention to dismantle its weapons of mass destruction completely and to limit the range of Libyan missiles to no greater than 300 kms, in accordance with the parameters set by the Missile Technology Control Regime.

The Libyan government has undertaken that this process will be transparent and verifiable. Libya will immediately adhere to the

Chemical Weapons Convention and conclude with the International Atomic Energy Agency an Additional Protocol to its Safeguards Agreement. We have offered our support to Libya in presenting its programmes to these international bodies and are prepared to offer assistance with dismantlement.

This decision by Colonel Qadhafi is an historic one. I applaud it. It will make the region and the world more secure. It shows that problems of proliferation can, with good will, be tackled through discussion and engagement, to be followed up by the responsible international agencies. It demonstrates that countries can abandon programmes voluntarily and peacefully. The Libyan government has stated that weapons of mass destruction are not the answer for Libya's defence. No more are they the answers for the region. Libya's actions entitle it to rejoin the international community. I have spoken to Colonel Qadhafi to say that, as the process of dismantlement goes forward, I now look forward to developing a productive relationship with him and with Libya.

Today's announcement is a further step in making the world a safer place. The UK, US and our partners are determined to stop the threat of WMD. We have played a leading role in the IAEA, with our closest allies, on the issue of Iran and nuclear weapons. We strongly support the Six Party talks on North Korea. We have enforced Security Council resolutions relating to Iraq. We have played a leading role in the Proliferation Security Initiative designed to interdict the passage of cargoes which could be used in WMD programmes. These actions show that we are serious about effective multilateral action against WMD.

And today's decisions show that recent events and political determination are opening up possibilities which just a few years ago would have been unthinkable. We must work now to create new partnerships, across geographical and cultural divides, backed by tough international rules and action.

We have identified the security threat of the early 21st century. It is the combination of terrorism and the development of nuclear or chemical or biological weapons of mass destruction.

September 11 showed the world this new form of terrorism knows no limits to the innocent lives it will take. WMD are the means by which it could destroy our world's security, and with it our way of life.

Today's announcement shows that we can fight this menace through more than purely military means; that we can defeat it peacefully, if countries are prepared, in good faith, to work with the international community to dismantle such weapons. Those countries who pursue such a path will find ready partners in the US and in the UK, as Libya will see. We never have wanted, as our opponents falsely claim, to dominate the world, to wage war on Muslims or Arabs, to interfere with the legitimate rights of sovereign nations.

We have only ever wanted to make peace in our world lasting and stable, built on sure foundations, peace for people of all faiths, all cultures, all nations who desire the good of their citizens and the wider world. Tonight is a further step on that journey.

## *Statement by President Bush:*

Good evening. I have called you here today to announce a development of great importance in our continuing effort to prevent the spread of weapons of mass destruction. Today in Tripoli, the leader of Libya, Colonel Moammar al-Ghadafi, publicly confirmed his commitment to disclose and dismantle all weapons of mass destruction programs in his country. He has agreed immediately and unconditionally to allow inspectors from international organizations to enter Libya. These inspectors will render an accounting of all nuclear, chemical and biological weapons programs and will help oversee their elimination. Colonel Ghadafi's commitment, once it is fulfilled, will make our country more safe and the world more peaceful.

Talks leading to this announcement began about nine months ago when Prime Minister Tony Blair and I were contacted through personal envoys by Colonel Ghadafi. He communicated to us his willingness to make a decisive change in the policy of his government. At the direction of Colonel Ghadafi, himself, Libyan officials have provided American and British officers with documentation on that country's chemical, biological, nuclear and ballistic missile programs and activities. Our experts in these fields have met directly with Libyan officials to learn additional details.

Opposing proliferation is one of the highest priorities of the war against terror. The attacks of September the 11th, 2001 brought tragedy to the United States and revealed a future threat of even greater magnitude. Terrorists who killed thousands of innocent people would, if they ever gained weapons of mass destruction, kill hundreds of thousands — without hesitation and without mercy. And this danger is dramatically increased when regimes build or acquire weapons of mass destruction and maintain ties to terrorist groups.

The United States and our allies are applying a broad and active strategy to address the challenges of proliferation, through diplomacy and through the decisive actions that are sometimes needed. We've enhanced our intelligence capabilities in order to trace dangerous weapons activities. We've organized a proliferation security initiative to interdict dangerous materials and technologies in transit. We've insisted on multilateral approaches like that in North Korea to confront threats. We are supporting the work of the International Atomic Energy Agency to hold the Iranian regime to its treaty obligations.

We obtained an additional United Nations Security Council Resolution requiring Saddam Hussein to prove that he had disarmed, and when that resolution was defied, we led a coalition to enforce it. All of these actions by the United States and our allies have sent an unmistakable message to regimes that seek or possess weapons of mass destruction. Those weapons do not bring influence or prestige. They bring isolation and otherwise unwelcome consequences.

And another message should be equally clear: leaders who abandon the pursuit of chemical, biological and nuclear weapons, and the means to deliver them, will find an open path to better relations with the United States and other free nations. With today's announcement by its leader, Libya has begun the process of rejoining the community of nations. And Colonel Ghadafi knows the way forward. Libya should carry out the commitments announced today. Libya should also fully engage in the war against terror. Its government, in response to the United Nations Security Council Lockerbie demands, has already renounced all acts of terrorism and pledged cooperation in the international fight against terrorism. We expect Libya to meet these commitments, as well.

As the Libyan government takes these essential steps and demonstrates its seriousness, its good faith will be returned. Libya can regain a secure and respected place among the nations, and over time, achieve far better relations with the United States. The

Libyan people are heirs to an ancient and respected culture, and their country lies at the center of a vital region. As Libya becomes a more peaceful nation, it can be a source of stability in Africa and the Middle East.

Should Libya pursue internal reform, America will be ready to help its people to build a more free and prosperous country. Great Britain shares this commitment, and Prime Minister Blair and I welcome today's declaration by Colonel Ghadafi. Because Libya has a troubled history with America and Britain, we will be vigilant in ensuring its government lives up to all its responsibilities. Yet, as we have found with other nations, old hostilities do not need to go on forever. And I hope that other leaders will find an example in Libya's announcement today.

Our understanding with Libya came about through quiet diplomacy. It is a result, however, of policies and principles declared to all. Over the last two years, a great coalition of nations has come together to oppose terror and to oppose the spread of weapons of mass destruction. We've been clear in our purposes. We have shown resolve. In word and in action, we have clarified the choices left to potential adversaries. And when leaders make the wise and responsible choice, when they renounce terror and weapons of mass destruction, as Colonel Ghadafi has now done, they serve the interest of their own people and they add to the security of all nations.

# ANNEX D

# Remarks by President George W. Bush at Oak Ridge National Laboratory, July 12, 2004

THE PRESIDENT: Thank you for the warm welcome. I realize the Y-12 National Security Complex doesn't get a lot of visitors -- so thanks for the special arrangements. I'm also glad to have the opportunity to thank each one of you for the vital work you do here. And please pass the word to your fellow employees, many of whom were waving, I want you to know, as we drove in, for which I'm thankful. The nation counts on your great expertise and your professionalism in producing, protecting, and maintaining material that is critical to our security. America is safer because of your service at Oak Ridge. You need to know our nation is grateful for that service.

I appreciate our Secretary of Energy Spence Abraham. He traveled with me today. Thank you, Mr. Secretary, for your service. I want to thank Jeffrey Wadsworth, who's the Director of Oak Ridge National Laboratory. It's not the first time I've met Jeffrey. I appreciate Jon Kreykes. I want to thank all the people who helped make this visit a successful visit. I want to thank Senator Lamar Alexander, the other members of the United States Congress who are traveling with us today -- strong supporters, by the way, of Oak Ridge. I appreciate the Mayor being here, David Bradshaw. Mr. Mayor, appreciate you taking time to come. I want to thank my fellow citizens for giving me a chance to come and visit.

I've just had a close look at some of the dangerous equipment secured in this place. Eight months ago, the centrifuge parts and processing equipment for uranium were 5,000 miles away in the nation of Libya. They were part of a secret nuclear weapons program. Today, Libya, America and the world are better off because these components are safely in your care.

These materials are the sobering evidence of a great danger. Certain regimes, often with ties to terrorist groups, seek the ultimate weapons as a shortcut to influence. These materials, voluntarily turned over by the Libyan government, are also encouraging evidence that nations can abandon those ambitions and choose a better way.

Libya is dismantling its weapons of mass destruction and long-range missile programs. This progress came about through quiet diplomacy between America, Britain and the Libyan government. This progress was set in motion, however, by policies declared in public to all the world. The United States, Great Britain, and many other nations are determined to expose the threats of terrorism and proliferation -- and to oppose those threats with all our power. We have sent this message in the strongest diplomatic terms, and we have acted where action was required.

Every potential adversary now knows that terrorism and proliferation carry serious consequences, and that the wise course is to abandon those pursuits. By choosing that course, the Libyan government is serving the interests of its own people and adding to the security of all nations.

America's determination to actively oppose the threats of our time was formed and fixed on September the 11th, 2001. On that day we saw the cruelty of the terrorists, and we glimpsed the future they intend for us. They intend to strike the United States to the limits of their power. They seek weapons of mass destruction to kill Americans on an even greater scale. And this danger is increased when outlaw regimes build or acquire weapons of mass destruction and maintain ties to terrorist groups.

This is our danger, but not our fate. America has the resources and the strength and the resolve to overcome this threat. We are waging a broad and unrelenting war against terror, and an active campaign against proliferation. We refuse to live in fear. We are making steady progress.

To protect our people, we're staying on the offensive against threats within our own country. We are using the Patriot Act to track terrorist activity and to break up terror cells. Intelligence and law enforcement officials are sharing information as never before. We've transformed the mission of the FBI to focus on preventing terrorism. Every element of our homeland security plan is critical, because the terrorists are ruthless and resourceful -- and we know they're preparing to attack us again. It's not possible to guarantee perfect security in our vast, free nation. But I can assure our fellow Americans, many fine professionals in intelligence and national security and homeland security and law enforcement are working around the clock doing everything they can to protect the country. And we're grateful to them all.

To overcome the dangers of our time, America is also taking a new approach in the world. We're determined to challenge new threats, not ignore them, or simply wait for future tragedy. We're helping to build a hopeful future in hopeless places, instead of allowing troubled regions to remain in despair and explode in violence. Our goal is a lasting, democratic peace, in which free nations are free from the threat of sudden terror. Our strategy for peace has three commitments: First, we are defending the peace by taking the fight to the enemy. We will confront them overseas so we do not have to confront them here at home. We are destroying the leadership of terrorist networks in sudden raids, disrupting their planning and financing, and keeping them on the run. Month by month, we are shrinking the space in which they can freely operate, by denying them territory and the support of governments.

Second, we're protecting the peace by working with friends and allies and international institutions to isolate and confront terrorists and outlaw regimes. America is leading a broad coalition of nations to disrupt proliferation. We're working with the United Nations, the International Atomic Energy Agency, and other inter-national organizations to take action in our common security. The global threat of terrorism requires a global response. To be effective, that global response requires leadership -- and America will lead.

Third, we are extending the peace by supporting the rise of democracy, and the hope and progress that democracy brings, as the alternative to hatred and terror in the broader Middle East. In democratic and successful societies, men and women do not swear allegiance to malcontents and murderers; they turn their hearts and labor to building better lives. And democratic governments do not shelter terrorist camps or attack their neighbors. When justice and democracy advance, so does the hope of lasting peace.

We have followed this strategy -- defending the peace, protecting the peace and extending the peace -- for nearly three years. We have been focused and patient, firm and consistent. And the results are all now clear to see.

Three years ago, the nation of Afghanistan was the home base of al Qaeda, a country ruled by the Taliban, one of the most backward and brutal regimes of modern history. Schooling was denied girls. Women were whipped in the streets and executed in a sports stadium. Millions lived in fear. With protection from the Taliban, al Qaeda and its associates trained, indoctrinated, and sent forth thousands of killers to set up terror cells in dozens of countries, including our own.

Today, Afghanistan is a world away from the nightmare of the Taliban. That country has a good and just President. Boys and girls are being educated. Many refugees have returned home to rebuild their country, and a presidential election is scheduled for this fall. The terror camps are closed and the Afghan government is helping us to hunt the Taliban and terrorists in remote regions. Today, because we acted to liberate Afghanistan, a threat has been removed, and the American people are safer.

Three years ago, Pakistan was one of the few countries in the world that recognized the Taliban regime. Al Qaeda was active and recruiting in Pakistan, and was not seriously opposed. Pakistan served as a transit point for al Qaeda terrorists leaving Afghanistan on missions of murder. Yet the United States was not on good terms with Pakistan's military and civilian leaders -- the very people we would need to help shut down al Qaeda operations in that part of the world.

Today, the governments of the United States and Pakistan are working closely in the fight against terror. President Musharraf is a friend of our country, who helped us capture Khalid Sheik Mohammed, the operational planner behind the September the 11th attacks. And Pakistani forces are rounding up terrorists along their nation's western border. Today, because we're working with the Pakistani leaders, Pakistan is an ally in the war on terror, and the American people are safer.

Three years ago, terrorists were well-established in Saudi Arabia. Inside that country, fundraisers and other facilitators gave al Qaeda financial and logistical help, with little scrutiny or opposition. Today, after the attacks in Riyadh and elsewhere, the Saudi government knows that al Qaeda is its enemy. Saudi Arabia is working hard to shut down the facilitators and financial supporters of terrorism. The government has captured or killed many first-tier leaders of the al Qaeda organization in Saudi Arabia -- including one last week. Today, because Saudi Arabia has seen the danger and has joined the war on terror, the American people are safer.

Three years ago, the ruler of Iraq was a sworn enemy of America, who provided safe haven for terrorists, used weapons of mass destruction, and turned his nation into a prison. Saddam Hussein was not just a dictator; he was a proven mass murderer who refused to account for weapons of mass murder. Every responsible nation recognized this threat, and knew it could not go on forever.

America must remember the lessons of September the 11th. We must confront serious dangers before they fully materialize. And so my administration looked at the intelligence on Iraq, and we saw a threat. Members of the United States Congress from both political parties looked at the same intelligence, and they saw a threat. The United Nations Security Council looked at the intelligence, and it saw a threat. The previous administration and the Congress looked at the intelligence and made regime change in Iraq the policy of our country.

In 2002, the United Nations Security Council yet again demanded a full accounting of Saddam Hussein's weapons programs. As he had for over a decade, Saddam Hussein refused to comply. In fact, according to former weapons inspector David Kay, Iraq's weapons programs were elaborately shielded by security and deception operations that continued even beyond the end of Operation Iraqi Freedom. So I had a choice to make: Either take the word of a madman, or defend America. Given that choice, I will defend America every time.

Although we have not found stockpiles of weapons of mass destruction, we were right to go into Iraq. We removed a declared enemy of America, who had the capability of producing weapons of mass murder, and could have passed that capability to terrorists bent on acquiring them. In the world after September the 11th, that was a risk we could not afford to take.

Today, the dictator who caused decades of death and turmoil, who twice invaded his neighbors, who harbored terrorist leaders, who used chemical weapons on innocent men, women, and children, is finally before the bar of justice. Iraq, which once had the worst government in the Middle East, is now becoming an example of reform to the region. And Iraqi security forces are fighting beside coalition troops to defeat the terrorists and foreign fighters who threaten their nation and the world. Today, because America and our coalition helped to end the violent regime of Saddam Hussein, and because we're helping to raise a peaceful democracy in its place, the American people are safer.

Three years ago, the nation of Libya, a longtime supporter of terror, was spending millions to acquire chemical and nuclear weapons. Today, thousands of Libya's chemical munitions have been destroyed. And nuclear processing equipment that could ultimately have threatened the lives of hundreds of thousands is stored away right here in Oak Ridge, Tennessee. Today, because the Libyan government saw the seriousness of the civilized world, and correctly judged its own interests, the American people are safer.

Three years ago, a private weapons proliferation network was doing business around the world. This network, operated by the Pakistani nuclear scientist, A. Q. Khan, was selling nuclear plans and equipment to the highest bidder, and found willing buyers in places like Libya, Iran, and North Korea. Today, the A. Q. Khan network is out of business. We have ended one of the most dangerous sources of proliferation in the world, and the American people are safer.

Breaking this proliferation network was possible because of the outstanding work done by the CIA. Dedicated intelligence officers were tireless in obtaining vital information, sometimes at great personal risk. Our intelligence services do an essential job for America. I thank them for their dedication and hard work. The Senate Intelligence Committee has identified some shortcomings in our intelligence capabilities; the Committee's report will help us in the work of reform. Our nation needs more intelligence agents -- what is called human intelligence -- to cover the globe. We must have the best, cutting-edge technology to listen and look for dangers. We must have better coordination among intelligence services. I need, and the Congress needs, the best possible intelligence in order to protect the American people. We're determined to make sure we get it.

Three years ago, the world was very different. Terrorists planned attacks, with little fear of discovery or reckoning. Outlaw regimes supported terrorists and defied the civilized world, without shame and with few consequences. Weapons proliferators sent their deadly shipments and grew wealthy, encountering few obstacles to their trade.

The world changed on September the 11th, and since that day, we have changed the world. We are leading a steady, confident, systematic campaign against the dangers of our time. There are still terrorists who plot against us, but the ranks of their leaders are thinning, and they know what fate awaits them. There are still regimes actively supporting the terrorists, but fewer than there used to be. There are still outlaw regimes pursuing weapons of mass destruction, but the world no longer looks the other way. Today, because America has acted, and because America has led, the forces of terror and tyranny have suffered defeat after defeat, and America and the world are safer.

All this progress has been achieved with the help of other responsible nations. The case of Libya's nuclear disarmament is a good example. In the fall of 2003, American and British intelligence were tracking a large shipment of nuclear equipment bound for Tripoli aboard a German-registered cargo ship. We alerted German and Italian authorities, who diverted the ship to an Italian port where the cargo was confiscated. We worked together. These events helped encourage Libya to reconsider its nuclear ambitions. That was a dramatic breakthrough, achieved by allies working together. And the cooperation of America's allies in the war on terror is very, very strong.

We're grateful to the more than 60 nations that are supporting the Proliferation Security Initiative to intercept illegal weapons and equipment by sea, land, and air. We're grateful to the more than 30 nations with forces serving in Iraq, and the nearly 40 nations with forces in Afghanistan. In the fight against terror, we've asked our allies to do hard things. They've risen to their responsibilities. We're proud to call them friends.

We have duties and there will be difficulties ahead. We're working with responsible governments and international institutions to convince the leaders of North Korea and Iran that their nuclear weapons ambitions are deeply contrary to their own interests. We're helping governments fight poverty and disease, so they do not become failed states and future havens for terror. We've launched our Broader Middle East Initiative, to encourage reform and democracy throughout the region, a project that will shape the history of our times for the better. We're working to build a free and democratic Palestinian state, which lives in peace with Israel and adds to the peace of the region. We're keeping our commitments to the people of Afghanistan and Iraq, who are building the world's newest democracies. They're counting on us to help. We will not abandon them. Delivering these nations from tyranny has required sacrifice and loss. We will honor that sacrifice by finishing the great work we have begun.

In this challenging period of our history, Americans fully understand the dangers to our country. We remain a nation at risk, directly threatened by an enemy that plots in secret to cause terrible harm and grief. We remain a nation at war, fighting for our security, our freedom, and our way of life. We also see our advantages clearly. Americans have a history of rising to every test; our generation is no exception. We've not forgotten September the 11th, 2001. We will not allow our enemies to forget it, either.

We have strong allies, including millions of people in the Middle East who want to live in freedom. And the ideals we stand for have a power of their own. The appeal of justice and liberty, in the end, is greater than the appeal of hatred and tyranny in any form. The war on terror will not end in a draw, it will end in a victory, and you and I will see that victory of human freedom.

I want to thank you all for coming. Thank you for your dedication. May God bless you and your families, and may God continue to bless our great country. Thank you very much.

# *INDEX*

Printed in the United States
135517LV00001B/10/P